AMISH CRIB QUILTS
FROM THE MIDWEST

The Sara Miller Collection

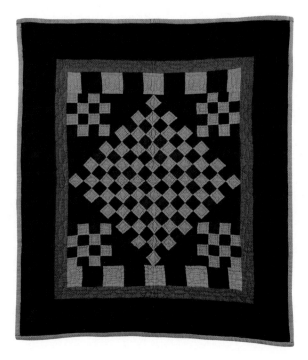

AMISH
CRIB QUILTS
FROM THE MIDWEST

The Sara Miller Collection

Janneken Smucker, Patricia Cox Crews,
& Linda Welters

International Quilt Study Center,
at the University of Nebraska-Lincoln
in cooperation with

Intercourse, PA 17534
800/762-7171 • www.goodbks.com

This publication and associated exhibition at the University of Nebraska-Lincoln were supported by funding from:
The National Endowment for the Humanities Challenge Grant
The Nebraska Humanities Council
The International Quilt Study Center at the University of Nebraska-Lincoln
The Center for Great Plains Studies, University of Nebraska-Lincoln

Published on the occasion of the exhibition:
"At the Crossing: Midwestern Amish Crib Quilts and the Intersection of Cultures"
Exhibition Curator: Janneken Smucker

Exhibition Itinerary:
The Great Plains Art Collection, Christlieb Gallery
University of Nebraska-Lincoln
Lincoln, Nebraska
February 14, 2003 to February 15, 2004

The People's Place Quilt Museum
Intercourse, Pennsylvania
March 21 to November 1, 2003

All photographs and catalog descriptions of the Sara Miller Collection quilts
© the International Quilt Study Center at the University of Nebraska-Lincoln

Quilt photography by John Nollendorfs

Figures 9, 14, and 19 by Jennifer Bailey, graphic designer at University of Nebraska-Lincoln

Design by Dawn J. Ranck

AMISH CRIB QUILTS FROM THE MIDWEST: THE SARA MILLER COLLECTION
Copyright © 2003 by Good Books, Intercourse, PA 17534
International Standard Book Number: 1-56148-389-3
Library of Congress Catalog Card Number: 2003040762

Library of Congress Cataloging-in-Publication Data
Smucker, Janneken.
    Amish crib quilts from the Midwest : the Sara Miller collection / Janneken
Smucker, Patricia Cox Crews & Linda Welters.
        p. cm.
    Exhibition itinerary: the Great Plains Art Collection, Christlieb Gallery, Univ. of
Nebraska-Lincoln, Lincoln, Neb., Feb. 14, 2003 to Feb. 15, 2004, the People's Place
Quilt Museum, Intercourse, Pa, March 21 to Nov. 1, 2003.
    Includes bibliographical references.
    ISBN 1-56148-389-3
    1. Crib quilts, Amish--Middle West--Exhibitions. 2. Miller, Sara--Art collections--
Exhibitions. 3. Quilts-- Private collections--Iowa--Kalona--Exhibitions. I. Crews,
Patricia Cox. II. Welters, Linda. III. Great Plains Art Collection. IV. People's Place
Quilt Museum (Intercourse, Pa.) V. Title.
NK9112.S6 2003
746.46'0437--dc21   2003040762

TABLE OF CONTENTS

ACKNOWLEDGMENTS

Many persons helped us to realize our vision of producing an exhibition and publication about Midwestern Amish crib quilts. First, thanks must go to Carolyn Ducey, Curator of the International Quilt Study Center (IQSC) Collections, for her outstanding dedication, enthusiasm, and hard work on virtually every aspect of this project, as well as a number of other projects ongoing at the IQSC. She capably planned and scheduled the volunteer staff who prepared the quilts for exhibition, and she thoughtfully read and offered advice on the book's descriptions at various stages. Those are just a few of the ways she assisted with this project.

Additional thanks must go to Marin Hanson, Assistant Curator, for her skillful help in preparing the final manuscript, organizing the photographic and electronic files of images, and massaging the electronic database for information we needed to write the captions and descriptions for each quilt featured here. Without her expert assistance, we never would have met our publication deadline.

Thanks also goes to the IQSC volunteer staff who helped in so many ways to prepare for the exhibition: Jean Ang, Irene Colburn, Beverly Cunningham, Jean Davie, Lauren Davis, Mary Ghormley, Jackie Greenfield, Pat Hackley, Judy Hess, Kathy Murphy, Nan Nelson, Louise Ripa, Judy Schwender, Stephanie Whitson, Lois Wilson, and Dorothy Wolfe.

Reese Summers, Curator of the Great Plains Art Collection at the University of Nebraska-Lincoln, enthusiastically agreed to a year-long exhibition of the Sara Miller Collection in the new Christlieb Gallery. His ideas for the installation, public programming, and publicity, promise to bring this remarkable collection and cultural tradition to a much broader audience. We extend our thanks to Stacey Walsh, Registrar for the Great Plains Art Collection, for her able assistance in a myriad of ways.

We are grateful to the staff at Good Books for their capable work in bringing this volume to publication. We extend a special thanks to Merle and Phyllis Good for their commitment to this project and willingness to make it a priority.

We are especially grateful to Robert and Ardis James, whose vision led to the formation of the International Quilt Study Center and whose generosity made it possible to bring the Sara Miller Collection to the University of Nebraska-Lincoln.

We extend our appreciation to the University of Nebraska-Lincoln Vice Chancellor for Academic Affairs Office, which awarded the Othmer Enhancement Funds that provided the stipend for Dr. Linda Welter's Visiting Faculty Fellowship.

Finally, we would like to acknowledge the support of the Nebraska Humanities Council and the National Endowment for the Humanities Challenge Grant, which provided financial support for the production of this book.

Patricia Cox Crews and
Janneken Smucker
International Quilt Study Center
University of Nebraska-Lincoln

THE INTERNATIONAL QUILT STUDY CENTER

The International Quilt Study Center (IQSC) at the University of Nebraska-Lincoln (UNL) was formed in 1997 as a result of the gift of nearly 950 quilts from Robert and Ardis James. The Jameses also pledged their financial support to create an endowment to support a center that encourages scholarship and nurtures the appreciation of quilts as art and cultural history. The University of Nebraska-Lincoln responded by building a state-of-the-art storage facility and funding scholarly positions to staff the academic center.

The mission of the IQSC is to encourage the interdisciplinary study of all aspects of quiltmaking traditions and to preserve this tradition through educational programs, coupled with collection, conservation, and exhibition of quilts and related materials. The IQSC holds the world's largest collection of quilts in public trust, a total of more than 1250 quilts. Three collections constitute the bulk of the IQSC's holdings: The Ardis and Robert James Collection, The Robert and Helen Cargo Collection of 156 African American quilts, and the Sara Miller Collection of 90 Amish crib quilts.

The IQSC in partnership with the UNL Department of Textiles, Clothing and Design offers a unique masters program in textile history with a quilt studies emphasis. The graduate program is designed for persons interested in analyzing the complex ways in which gender, class, ethnicity, aesthetics, politics, religion, and technology find expression in textile arts, quiltmaking traditions, design, and culture. Graduates of the degree programs are prepared for careers or career advancement in museums, historic houses, galleries, auction houses, and government agencies in the areas of collection care and management, education, and research. Students may complete the program entirely in residence or may elect to participate in the "hybrid" distance delivery program, which allows them to complete the program with only one semester of residency on the University of Nebraska-Lincoln campus.

To encourage scholarship, the IQSC also offers Visiting Faculty Fellowships and sponsors a biennial symposium. The Visiting Faculty Fellowships awarded annually bring outstanding scholars to campus to research the collection and interact with students and faculty associated with the IQSC. The biennial symposium brings scholars from around the world to participate in dialogue regarding the artistic, social, and cultural history of quiltmaking and related textile traditions worldwide.

Patricia Cox Crews, Ph.D.
Director and Professor
International Quilt Study Center
Department of Textiles, Clothing and Design
University of Nebraska-Lincoln

Fans
Maker unknown
1910-1930
Probably made in Indiana
(See Plate 61 for more information)

INTRODUCTION

by Patricia Cox Crews

Amish quilts, in general, and Amish crib quilts, in particular, represent a unique tradition within the broader context of American arts and crafts. Amish quilts in crib and youth-bed sizes are not made with the frequency that full-sized Amish quilts are made, despite the relatively large families common within Amish society. Collectors, dealers, scholars, and quilt aficionados appreciate Amish quilts for their visual qualities and exceptionally fine needlework, but some collectors especially prize the so-called crib quilts made by Amish women because of their rarity and special status. Therefore, I was intrigued when a collection of *90* Amish crib quilts was offered to the International Quilt Study Center (IQSC) by Xenia Cord, owner of an antique quilts brokerage in Kokomo, Indiana. The collection had been assembled by Sara Miller from Kalona, Iowa, a woman who had spent much of her life as a member of the Old Order Amish church.

Our surprise at being offered such a unique collection prompted us to engage Darwin Bearley to survey and evaluate the Miller Collection. Bearley, an antique quilt dealer located in Akron, Ohio, owns a personal collection of Amish crib quilts numbering about 50. He expressed surprise that he had never heard of the Amish woman who assembled such a large collection of crib quilts. After viewing the collection, he stated that he believed all were authentic and that the quality in general was "extremely high." He felt that a number of the crib quilts were "very unusual and unique ones." With the Sara Miller Collection of Amish crib quilts vetted, Robert and Ardis James generously

decided to acquire the remarkable collection on behalf of the IQSC in September, 2000, preserving it for future generations to study and enjoy.

The Miller Collection consists of 90 Amish crib quilts, dating from the early 1900s to the 1960s. With single-minded purpose and a discerning eye, Sara Miller assembled this extraordinary collection. She occupies a unique position among collectors of Amish quilts. She is one of the few insiders (possibly the only insider) who has amassed a collection of Amish quilts, and the only collector affiliated with the Amish who has assembled a collection of crib quilts, so far as we can tell.

Soon after we acquired the Miller Collection, IQSC Curator Carolyn Ducey and I began to explore possible venues for an exhibition on the University of Nebraska-Lincoln campus. Since most of the Miller quilts were believed to have a Midwestern provenance, we decided to approach Reese Summers, Curator of the Great Plains Art Collection. He responded with enthusiasm and a willingness to devote one part of the new Christlieb Gallery for an entire year to the proposed exhibition. As planning progressed for the future exhibition, we determined that it would not be possible to display all 90 quilts at one time in the Great Plains Art Collection Christlieb Gallery. At the same time, it was the firm belief of Reese Summers that the exhibition would have greater appeal to audiences if all 90 quilts were displayed. Therefore, we decided to display 22 to 23 quilts at a time, with a new group every three months, so that visitors could see the entire col-

Plate 1
Tumbling Blocks
Maker unknown • 1920-1940 • Possibly made in Indiana • 44.5" x 35" • Cottons • QSPI: 6-7
International Quilt Study Center, Sara Miller Collection, 2000.007.0078

The Tumbling Blocks pattern often produces a visual illusion in which three-dimensional blocks tilt out at the viewer. This sensation is created by placing the 60-degree diamonds in orderly rows based on value contrast. This quiltmaker departed from that formula and arranged the diamonds randomly. The lack of pattern causes the viewer's eye to jump from diamond to diamond, searching for a place to rest.

lection by returning to view each of the four rotations between February 2003 and February 2004.

Fortuitously, about the time that preliminary planning began for the future exhibition of the Miller Collection, a new graduate student, Janneken Smucker, entered the University of Nebraska's masters program in textile history with a quilt studies emphasis. She expressed an interest in undertaking the curatorial research for the exhibition as her masters project. Researching the Miller Collection and serving as exhibition curator matched Janneken's background, education, and interests: Janneken Smucker is of Mennonite background and is a graduate in history and women's studies from Goshen (Indiana) College, a small Mennonite liberal arts college. Not only is she descended from a line of quiltmakers, she is a quiltmaker herself. Her educational and religious background (both the Amish and the Mennonites are Germanic sectarian religious groups) provided her with special insights into the Amish culture, thereby enriching her research of the collection and informing her thoughtful essay in this volume.

Another fortuitous circumstance, which further contributed to the scholarship of this project, was Dr. Linda Welters' application for an IQSC Visiting Faculty Fellowship. Dr. Welters is Professor of Textiles, Fashion Merchandising and Design at the University of Rhode Island. She proposed to apply symmetry analysis to the Sara Miller Collection of Amish crib quilts. Symmetry analysis can be applied to repeating patterns found in nature and human artifacts. The model for symmetry analysis that Welters proposed to use was set forth by Dorothy Washburn and Donald Crowe in *Symmetries of Culture: Theory and Practice of Plane Pattern Analysis.* They demonstrate how preferences for particular symmetry patterns offer clues to cultural beliefs and practices, including aspects of group identity and cultural contact. Welters argued persuasively that quilts with their repeating block patterns were well suited to meaningful symmetry analysis. She further noted that, "Connecting quilts to cultural patterns requires a substantial number of quilts from a culture or region. The 90 Amish crib quilts in the Sara Miler Collection at the University of Nebraska-Lincoln offer

(continued on page 11)

Plate 2
Double Irish Chain
Maker unknown
1940-1960
Possibly made in Wisconsin
52" x 37.5"
Cottons
QSPI: 7-8
International Quilt Study Center,
Sara Miller Collection, 2000.007.0039

Amish settlers first arrived in Wisconsin in 1925, coming from other communities throughout the Midwest with the desire to establish a church with more conservative practices. For this reason, quilts made in (or acquired in) Wisconsin are difficult to distinguish from those made in other Midwestern Amish communities. By moving to a more isolated community, these Amish sought to remove themselves from the increasing modernization occurring in the more established Amish settlements elsewhere in the Midwest. In recent decades, Wisconsin has seen a boom in new Amish settlements, with more than 25 established at present.

Plate 3
Hole in the Barn Door
Mrs. Levi Bontrager • 1920-1940 • Probably made in Indiana • 55" x 36.5"
Cottons • QSPI: 8-9
International Quilt Study Center, Sara Miller Collection, 2000.007.0057

The 24 blocks in this quilt are pieced from a total of 10 different brown and 11 different blue fabrics of similar shades. The fabrics are made from a variety of weaves, including plain, basket, and twill. The quiltmaker achieved a fairly consistent look to the blocks, despite piecing from a variety of shades and fabric constructions.

Plate 4
Strip
Maker unknown • 1910-1930 • Made in Midwestern United States • 42.5" x 35"
Cottons • QSPI: 5-6
International Quilt Study Center, Sara Miller Collection, 2000.007.0055

This strip quilt combines Bow Tie and Flying Geese patterns. Perhaps these pieced strips were left over from piecing full-size quilts. On the other hand, maybe the quiltmaker chose this combination of patterns as a resourceful means of utilizing scraps left over from dressmaking. Regardless, surface soil and an abraded binding indicate that this quilt was well used.

Plate 5
Railroad Crossing
Maker unknown • 1910-1930 • Probably made in Ohio • 73.5" x 42" • Cottons • QSPI: 7-8
International Quilt Study Center, Sara Miller Collection, 2000.007.0016

The Railroad Crossing pattern, a favorite of the Ohio Amish, serves as a symbol for one of the recurring themes in this collection of quilts: the intersection of cultures. The Amish community often intersects with mainstream American society and is forced to make choices, as a community, about how to interact with this larger society while remaining true to their own beliefs. The bright yellow patch that pops out of the design field of squares reiterates another theme: that innovation by individuals exists, despite the high value placed upon conformity within Amish society.

such an opportunity." The Fellows of the International Quilt Study Center voted unanimously to award her the Visiting Faculty Fellowship for 2002-2003. Her intriguing essay for this volume is the product of her research at the IQSC.

Carolyn Ducey and I anticipated that the exhibition would be of interest to other museums, and, indeed, that proved to be the case. Merle and Phyllis Good, owners of Good Books and directors/curators of The People's Place Quilt Museum in Intercourse, Lancaster County, Pennsylvania, visited the IQSC during September, 2002, to explore the possibility of future exhibitions and publications in partnership with the IQSC. After learning more about the planned exhibition of the Miller Collection, they immediately expressed an interest in serving as a venue for the Midwestern Amish crib quilt exhibition and in publishing the accompanying book. The timing of their initial visit could not have been better. We are very pleased that in March, 2003, the first of two rotations of this exhibition will travel to The People's Place Quilt Museum, a museum devoted to the exhibition of antique Amish and Mennonite quilts. Located in Lancaster County, Pennsylvania, The People's Place Quilt Museum prom-

ises to bring the Sara Miller Collection to the attention of appreciative visitors and residents of the oldest existing Amish settlement in the United States.

An Overview of the Sara Miller Collection

The Sara Miller Collection of 90 Amish crib quilts appears to be largely of Midwestern origin—Ohio (26 quilts), Indiana (15), Iowa (14), Illinois (10), Kansas (6), Wisconsin (4), Michigan (2), and Pennsylvania (1), with the remaining (12) of Midwestern origin, but the particular state and settlement of each is unknown. We have little provenance (name of maker and sequence of ownership) for the quilts because Sara Miller purchased most of the quilts from a dealer, Steve Evans, who only rarely provided the makers' names; however, he usually supplied the name of the Amish settlement where he acquired the quilt. Although Sara Miller was sometimes disappointed by his unwillingness to supply the quiltmaker's family name, she continued to buy quilts from him because of the excellent examples he regularly brought to her for consideration.

The quilts range from crib size (the smallest of which is 29 x 28 inches—see Plate 6) to youth-bed size (the

(continued on page 15)

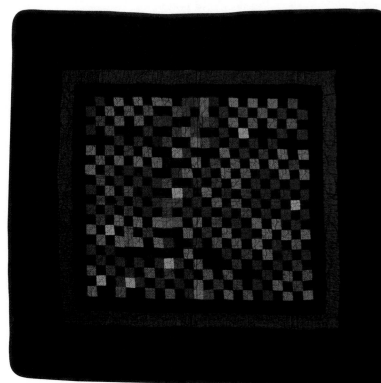

Plate 6
One Patch
Maker unknown
1920-1940
Possibly made in Holmes County, Ohio
29.5" x 28"
Cottons
QSPI: 7-8
International Quilt Study Center,
Sara Miller Collection, 2000.007.0064

The design field of this quilt is pieced from 460 three-quarter inch squares, some of which are pieced from more than one bit of fabric. Its diminutive dimensions make it the smallest quilt in the Miller Collection. Quilts in the collection range in size from very small, like this quilt, to oblong ones, likely used to cover youth beds or daybeds. Sara Miller says that children's quilts were made in all sizes, for use ranging from covering a newborn's cradle to a youth's three-quarter size bed.

Plate 7
Nine Patch
Mrs. Joe Gingerich • 1930-1950 • Probably made in Wayne County, Ohio • 40" x 35"
Cottons • QSPI: 6-7
International Quilt Study Center, Sara Miller Collection, 2000.007.0014

Unlike many other quilts in the Miller Collection, this quilt is simply a smaller version of a full-size Amish quilt. Rather than using the more typical two- or three-inch squares to create each Nine Patch, each square is less than one inch wide. The violet blocks placed in the corners provide the only significant contrast in value on this predominantly blue and black quilt.

Plate 8
Sunshine and Shadow
Maker unknown • 1920-1940 • Made in Midwestern United States • 31.5" x 27"
Cottons • QSPI: 6-8
International Quilt Study Center, Sara Miller Collection, 2000.007.0053

As part of the armistice settlement following World War I, American chemical companies received prized German patents for many synthetic dyes, which had not previously been produced in the United States. Many of the bright cheerful colors that were used by mainstream, and eventually Amish, quiltmakers in the twentieth century, such as those found in this quilt, were a result of the increased availability of synthetic dyes developed in Germany.

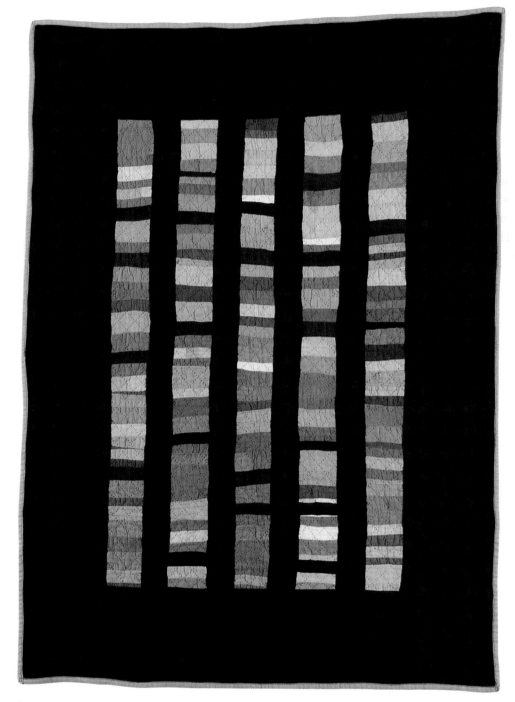

Plate 9
Chinese Coins
Maker unknown • 1930-1950 • Made in Midwestern United States;
acquired in Clark, Missouri • 45" x 33" • Cottons • QSPI: 6
International Quilt Study Center, Sara Miller Collection, 2000.007.0042

    This quilt is one of a handful from the Miller Collection that was acquired in Clark, Missouri. The geographic origin of the quilt is unknown because it was likely made prior to the settlement's founding in 1954. This settlement was not the first community founded by Amish in Missouri, although some earlier settlements became Amish-Mennonite, rather than remaining Old Order, following the years of division in the mid- to late-nineteenth century.

largest of which is 73 x 42 inches—see Plate 5), with most quilts in the 30+ x 30+, or 30+ x 40+ inches-range. A few are made from fine dress wool fabrics associated with the classic Amish quiltmaking tradition of Lancaster County, Pennsylvania. Others are made from solid-colored cottons typical of Midwestern Amish quilts. And, many are made of a combination of wool and cotton fabrics.

Many of the quilts are made in patterns typical of full-sized Amish quilts—Bars, Chinese Coins, Nine Patch, and Sunshine and Shadow. Others, however, are departures from the mainstream of Amish quiltmaking in a variety of ways. These interesting variances are examined in more detail in the descriptions accompanying each quilt and in Janneken Smucker's informative essay.

The plate captions for each quilt include basic information: pattern name, quiltmaker name when known, probable settlement or state where the quilt is believed to have been made, estimated date range, dimensions, quilting stitches per inch, and predominant fiber types. Since the Sara Miller Collection quilts are without verifiable provenance, we usually know only where each quilt was acquired. Given the mobile society of American quiltmakers, including Amish quiltmakers, we cannot assume that the community where it was acquired is the community where it was made. Therefore, Janneken Smucker very conservatively identified a place of origin for each quilt.

If we know only where a quilt was acquired, its place of origin was designated as "possibly" made in the settlement and/or state where it was acquired, unless the location appears to be an unreasonable possibility. For example, we realized that none of the quilts acquired in Clark, Missouri, could have been made there because the Clark, Missouri, Amish settlement was established after the dates by when we estimated the quilts were made. Therefore, we designated origin as "Made in the Midwestern United States; Acquired in Clark, Missouri," for those quilts. If a quilt exhibited identifiable characteristics of the particular Midwestern Amish community or state where it was acquired by the dealer, we designated it as "probably" having been made in the given settlement and/or state and discussed those distinguishing characteristics in

Plate 10
Log Cabin, Barn Raising variation
Maker unknown
1930-1950
Possibly made in Indiana;
acquired in Clark, Missouri
57.5" x 40"
Cottons
QSPI: 7
International Quilt Study Center,
Sara Miller Collection, 2000.007.0033

Log Cabin quilts, popular among many American quiltmakers, have numerous setting variations. In this Barn Raising design, there are two square "hearth" blocks at the center of each Log Cabin block instead of just one. This technique is a common practice among Indiana Amish quiltmakers, although it is uncertain where this quilt was made.

Plate 11
Log Cabin, Bull's Eye variation
Maker unknown • 1900-1920 • Possibly made in Holmes County, Ohio • 42" x 34.5"
Top: wools, wool/cotton mixtures, cottons; back and binding: cottons • QSPI: 7-8
International Quilt Study Center, Sara Miller Collection, 2000.007.0009

These Log Cabin blocks feature variously colored fine wools and wool/cotton mixtures. In all but three of the blocks, the colored strips alternate with black wool crepe. The remaining three blocks contain a variety of black fabrics, including sateen and plain weave cottons. Whereas most Log Cabin quilts are pieced to showcase an overall quilt design (see Plates 10 and 47 for Barn Raising and Straight Furrow examples), the individual Log Cabin blocks in this quilt are separated by green crepe sashing. Notice that one red Log Cabin block is pieced without the standard arrangement of "logs," perhaps in order to make this fabric stretch further.

16

the description. If we have no information about where a quilt was acquired, we simply designated it as made in the Midwest.

Since we also do not know with certainty when each quilt was made, the estimated date provided by the dealer or collector was our starting point. We sought additional stylistic clues to corroborate or refute those estimated dates. We chose to conservatively assign a span for the probable date of manufacture, generally a range of at least two decades. All appear to have been made between the early 1900s and the early 1960s.

The number of quilting stitches per inch (QSPI) is given for each quilt. It is the IQSC's standard protocol to count quilting stitches in at least three places. When it varies, we list the range rather than the average because the range is more telling. When quilting stitches vary widely, it suggests that more than one hand was involved in the quilting. It may also indicate that one hand was more experienced than another. Most of these quilts averaged six to eight quilting stitches per inch. Only one quilt (see Plate 43) averaged more than 10 quilting stitches per inch—an impressive 10-11 QSPI.

The fiber content also is given for each quilt top. The predominant fiber is listed first, followed by other fibers if present. Visual examination provided the basis for this information initially. Janneken Smucker performed microscopic analysis to corroborate visual assessment whenever particular fabrics used in a quilt appeared to be different from the predominant fiber type.

Cotton predominated in the majority (66) of the quilt tops in the Miller Collection. This was not surprising, as others have noted that cotton fabrics were used more often by Midwestern Amish women in their full-sized quilts than was customary for the Lancaster County Amish. Frequently, Janneken discovered that quilts designated as being made entirely of wool fabrics by the dealer or collector were, in fact, made of wools, wool/cotton mixtures, and sometimes cotton fabrics, as well. In fact, only two quilts in the entire collection proved to have tops made entirely from wool fabrics; one from Ohio (see Plate 12) and one from Iowa (see Plate 13). The only quilt acquired in Pennsylvania (see Plate 78) is made entirely of cottons, but

Plate 12
Zigzag
Maker unknown
1900-1920
Possibly made in Holmes County, Ohio
49" x 42"
Top: wools; back and binding: cottons
QSPI: 6-8
International Quilt Study Center,
Sara Miller Collection, 2000.007.0035

Like many others in the Miller Collection, this quilt is striking not only because of its design, but because of its fine workmanship. While a similar design pieced on a full-size quilt would be visually appealing, the scale of this quilt and the use of 1.5-inch rectangles make it all the more remarkable. Lighter-weight cotton fabrics would have allowed more ease in piecing such an intricate design, rather than the heavier wools that this quiltmaker chose.

17

Plate 13
Strip
Maker unknown • 1910-1930 • Possibly made in Johnson County, Iowa • 46.5" x 36"
Top: wools; back and binding: cottons • QSPI: 4-5
International Quilt Study Center, Sara Miller Collection, 2000.007.0004

Wool was used less often than cotton by most Midwestern Amish quiltmakers. According to Sara Miller, Midwestern Amish women often sewed their wedding dresses from fine dress wools. Leftover scraps from special-occasion dressmaking were in turn used to piece brightly colored quilts such as this one.

Plate 14
Sunshine and Shadow
Maker unknown
1940-1960
Possibly made in Oelwein, Iowa
45.5" x 36.5"
Cottons, a bit of wool
QSPI: 6-8
International Quilt Study Center,
Sara Miller Collection, 2000.007.0036

Two unique features are found on this Sunshine and Shadow quilt. First, an unusual fabric choice for Amish quilts—bright Kelly green-colored corduroy—is found among the patches. Second, the quilting stitches in the outside border form paired birds holding garlands of ribbons. Few Midwestern Amish quilts feature such representational quilting designs.

it is from Somerset County, located in southwestern Pennsylvania, rather than Lancaster County.

A number of quilts designated as all cotton contain pieces of wool fabrics or wool/cotton mixtures; sometimes there are only a few pieces, and in others there are a large number of pieces. We were surprised at the number of wool/cotton mixtures (fabrics with a cotton warp and wool weft, or vice versa) found in these Midwestern Amish quilts. Since few authors of other Amish quilt exhibition catalogues have performed microscopic analysis to confirm fiber content, we now wonder whether or not the classic Lancaster Amish quilts featured in so many of them are made entirely of wool, as usually designated. If Lancaster Amish quilts prior to the 1930s are made entirely of wool, then the presence of wool/cotton mixtures might serve as a useful distinguishing characteristic of Midwestern Amish quilts.

We hope that the careful examination, documentation, and descriptions provided for each quilt in this book, coupled with the informative and instructive essays, will enlarge and strengthen the existing body of knowledge about the extraordinary quiltmaking traditions of Amish women.

Plate 15
Railroad Crossing
Maker unknown • 1900-1920 • Possibly made in Ohio • 39" x 37"
Top: wools, wool/cotton mixtures; back: cotton • QSPI: 6-7
International Quilt Study Center, Sara Miller Collection, 2000.007.0013

The fabrics in this quilt serve as a swatchbook of dress wools and wool/cotton mixtures that were early favorites of Amish quiltmakers. Unlike Lancaster County Amish quiltmakers, who almost exclusively pieced with wool, Midwestern Amish quiltmakers preferred cotton by the early twentieth century. The use of wool, along with the curved corners of the binding (another indication of a late nineteenth-century or early twentieth-century date), suggests that this quilt is likely one of the oldest quilts in the Miller Collection.

AT THE CROSSING:

Midwestern Amish Crib Quilts and the Intersection of Cultures

by Janneken Smucker

Sara Miller, a woman affiliated with the Amish church for most of her life, assembled this collection of Midwestern Amish crib quilts while owning and operating a successful fabric and quilt shop in Kalona, Iowa, the home of the largest Amish settlement west of the Mississippi. The quilts were all acquired and likely made in various Amish settlements scattered across the Midwest.[1] In addition to providing the viewer with visual delight, quilts from the Sara Miller Collection of Amish crib quilts serve as documents that can reveal much about Midwestern Amish culture and about the many points where mainstream American culture intersects with Amish culture.

The patterns and the construction of the crib quilts themselves exemplify the cultural adaptation and interaction with mainstream society which the Amish have experienced during their North American existence. In the past 70 years, another plane of intersection has arisen as members of mainstream American society have developed an active fascination with Amish culture. The popularity of Amish quilts with both quilt collectors and the general public is an indicator of this attraction to a cultural group so distinct from the mainstream.

Miller's relationship with these quilts, and her interaction with mainstream American culture as a result of her quilt collection and fabric shop, are other examples of the interaction between the two cultures. Before these cultural intersections can be explored, we must first consider the historical background of the Old Order Amish and how they came to live in settlements throughout the Midwest.

During the Protestant Reformation of sixteenth-century Europe, the Anabaptists, some of whom became known as Swiss Brethren, and then later Mennonites, emerged as a radical religious group. Mennonites sought a strict separation of church and state, practiced voluntary adult baptism rather than infant baptism, and refused to participate in the military because it ran counter to their view of Christ's teachings of peaceful nonviolence.[2]

The Amish separated from the Mennonites in seventeenth-century Europe as a result of differences in discipline practices. Those desiring a stricter practice of shunning church members who digressed from the group, among other differences, were led by Jacob Amman, for whom the Amish were named. Amish groups began migrating to eastern Pennsylvania in the eighteenth century to seek relief from the religious persecution and economic hardships of Europe. The first Amish settlement in North America was founded in the mid-eighteenth century in Berks County, Pennsylvania. A second settlement followed soon thereafter in Lancaster County. Throughout the late eighteenth and nineteenth centuries, groups of Amish, some of them immigrants directly from Europe, began to form settlements further west.

Plate 16
Hole in the Barn Door
Maker unknown • 1900-1920 • Possibly made in Indiana • 33" x 37"
Wools, cottons, wool/cotton mixtures • QSPI: 6-7
International Quilt Study Center, Sara Miller Collection, 2000.007.0071

This quiltmaker effectively utilized a variety of fabrics to piece her Hole in the Barn Door quilt. Of particular note is the array of colors used to create the sashing between the blocks. A wine-colored border frames this hodgepodge of fabrics. One strip of velveteen is used, a very unusual touch for an Amish quilt.

Figure 1

Major Amish Settlements[3]
(including smaller settlements where Miller quilts were made or acquired)

Settlement	Year Founded
Lancaster Co., Pennsylvania	c.1760
Somerset Co., Pennsylvania	c.1772
Mifflin Co., Pennsylvania	1791
Holmes-Wayne-Tuscarawas Cos., Ohio	1808
Elkhart-Lagrange Cos., Indiana	1841
Johnson-Washington Cos., (Kalona) Iowa	1846
Arthur, Illinois	1864
Reno County (Haven, Hutchinson), Kansas	1883
Plain City, Ohio	1896
Centreville, Michigan	1910
Medford, Wisconsin	1925
Clark, Missouri	1954
Camden, Michigan	1956

From the mid-nineteenth century on, a slow sorting-out process, or gradual schism, occurred, with those Amish most resistant to change emerging as the "Old Order Amish."[4] The other group that developed at this time was known as the Amish-Mennonites. Eventually, many Amish-Mennonites became affiliated with the Mennonite Church, which today is among the more progressive groups within the Anabaptist faith family.

The term "Amish" now generally refers to the Old Order Amish. Throughout the twentieth century, Amish groups have continued to migrate and form new communities, as well as abandon unsuccessful settlements. At present, well over 200 Amish settlements exist in North America, although the majority of Amish live in or near the three largest settlements in Holmes County, Ohio, Lancaster County, Pennsylvania, and Elkhart and Lagrange Counties, Indiana.[5] New Amish communities are settled almost annually, and a majority of currently existing Amish settlements have been established since 1970.[6] The desire for affordable farmland has spurred the foundation of some new settlements. Some Amish have chosen to migrate to states more

Plate 17
Triangles
Maker unknown
1930-1950
Possibly made in Holmes County, Ohio
68" x 44.5"
Cottons
QSPI: 6-7
International Quilt Study Center,
Sara Miller Collection, 2000.007.0003

The dimensions of this quilt indicate that it was likely used on a youth-size bed or to cover a narrow daybed, often found in the parlors of Amish homes in place of upholstered sofas. The maker constructed it from paired triangles that form concentric rings radiating outward from the center of the quilt. Each ring is pieced with a unique two-color combination of triangles.

23

Plate 18
Log Cabin, Courthouse Steps variation
Maker unknown • 1900-1920
Made in Midwestern United States • 41" x 32" • Cottons • QSPI: 5-6
International Quilt Study Center, Sara Miller Collection, 2000.007.0059

Soft purple contrasts with a lustrous gold fabric to heighten the visual impact of this well-worn Log Cabin quilt. The maker pieced the hearth squares with red fabric, the traditional choice for the center of Log Cabin blocks. The quilt was heavily used, evident from the many mended areas found on it.

conducive to the Amish education practice of stopping formal schooling after the eighth grade. Other settlements have been founded to establish a more conservative or more liberal church discipline.

Amish history is filled with major and minor schisms, and migration has often been a reaction to religious disagreements.[7] Each settlement develops its own interpretation of the *Ordnung*, those rules, some written but many unwritten, that guide all aspects of Amish living, including dress-styles, church services, and farming practices.

Amish Adaptation

At first glance, the Amish may appear to be a fossilized culture trapped in another time. A closer examination of Amish culture reveals that it, like the rest of American society, has evolved and adapted over time. Unlike the fast-paced change of mainstream society, the Amish have been slower to change and are often more deliberate in their adaptation of new technologies. Sociologist Marc Olshan is quick to point out that "traditional Amish culture is as much a product of the encroaching world as it is a reflection of the beliefs, values, and practices of an earlier, more pristine era."[8]

The Amish may adapt aspects of mainstream society for themselves, such as new technology and quilt patterns, but they do so on their own terms. For example, the *Ordnung* in most Amish church districts prohibits installing telephones in Amish homes, but members may use telephones belonging to "English" (as the Amish refer to the non-Amish) neighbors or phones kept in "telephone shanties," booths resembling outhouses that are often placed at the end of a lane away from handy access.[9] Similarly, the tractor is generally forbidden for fieldwork on Amish farms, but farmers may use the tractor around the barn in "selective and controlled ways . . . such as blowing silage, grinding and mixing feed, and providing hydraulic power."[10] Amish farmers will also use a tractor-like engine, mounted on a four-wheel cart and pulled by a horse, to operate farm implements.[11] Such examples show how the Amish have practiced selective adaptation, a borrowing from mainstream culture coupled with maintenance of Amish sensibilities.

Plate 19
Chinese Coins
Maker unknown
1910–1930
Possibly made in Holmes County, Ohio
39.5" x 31.5"
Cottons
QSPI: 7
International Quilt Study Center,
Sara Miller Collection, 2000.007.0019

The Chinese Coin pattern may be an adaptation of the traditional Amish Bars pattern (see Plate 80), allowing the quiltmaker to use smaller pieces of fabric instead of the longer pieces of fabric required to piece the Bars design. This maker alternated indigo blue fabric with pink and red pieces to form the stacks of "coins" that are framed by a field of green cotton sateen.

25

Plate 20
North Carolina Lily
Maker unknown • 1920-1940 • Possibly made in Ohio • 46" x 34.5"
Wools, cottons, wool/cotton mixtures • QSPI: 7
International Quilt Study Center, Sara Miller Collection, 2000.007.0074

Both the North Carolina Lily and Baskets patterns feature representational designs that would not have been in the accepted repertoire of early Amish quiltmakers. Eventually some Amish quiltmakers adapted these patterns, as well as techniques to make them to fit their Amish sensibilities. Rather than using hidden hand-appliqué stitches, these two quiltmakers machine-appliquéd the lily stems and basket handles to the ground fabric. The prominent dark machine stitches reinforce the Amish value of humility; fancy hidden appliqué stitches may have been considered prideful (see also Plate 21).

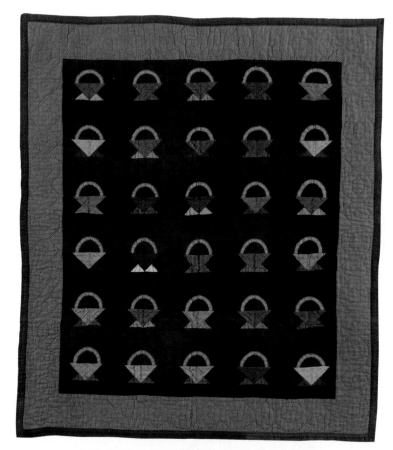

Plate 21
Baskets
Maker unknown
1920-1940
Possibly made in Hutchinson, Kansas
36" x 31.5"
Cottons
QSPI: 7
International Quilt Study Center,
Sara Miller Collection, 2000.007.0088

(See Plate 20)

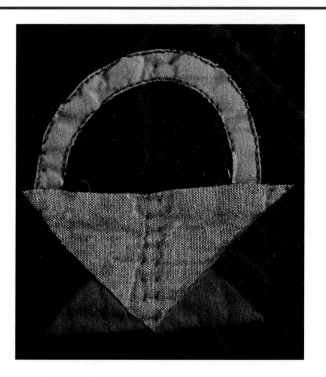

Figure 2

Detail of Basket quilt shown in Plate 21. Notice the machine appliqué method used to attach the blue handle.

Similar adaptation is found in Amish quiltmaking practices. For example, appliqué, the technique of sewing a decorative piece of fabric on top of a base fabric, often to create a representational design not possible by piecing geometric shapes together, was not often used by Amish quiltmakers because of a traditional prohibition against representational images (the same reason Amish shy away from photography). Amish quiltmakers may have considered the practice wasteful to cover up one layer of fabric with a second. But some quiltmakers, in their adaptation of borrowed "English" patterns (see Plates 20 and 21), modified the appliqué technique in order to create flower stems and basket handles. Rather than adopting the mainstream practice of using tiny, hidden appliqué stitches, these quiltmakers machine-stitched the stems and handles down with dark thread and left the edges of the appliquéd pieces raw, as seen in Figure 2. This approach kept the quiltmaker free from the sins of pride and wastefulness, but allowed her to use the pattern that required appliqué.

Unlike the Amish in Lancaster County, Pennsylvania, many Amish living in communities throughout the

27

Plate 22
Stars
Maker unknown • 1900-1920 • Possibly made in Hutchinson, Kansas • 45" x 39"
Cottons • QSPI: 7-8
International Quilt Study Center, Sara Miller Collection, 2000.007.0005

A variety of pieced patterns, and a seemingly random placement of blues, browns, and tans, crowd the design field of this Kansas quilt. Amish from Indiana, Iowa, and Illinois first began to settle in Kansas in 1883 and were among the many pioneers who ventured to the Great Plains in search of land and prosperity. Land agents placed advertisements in newspapers and almanacs read by the Amish to entice them to move west to Kansas.

Midwest migrated from settlement to settlement and often had more interaction with their non-Amish neighbors. Midwestern Amish groups' more frequent interaction with "the world" and their adventurous mindset (as reflected by their willingness to migrate more frequently) contributed to quiltmaking practices that were significantly different from those of the Lancaster County Amish. Lancaster Amish produced what are often regarded as the classic Amish quilts, featuring large fields of rich, contrasting colors in a center medallion format, pieced from fine wools with intricate quilting designs covering the ground (see Figure 4, page 37). Midwestern Amish, in contrast, adapted the quiltmaking vernacular of mainstream American quiltmakers, who by the mid-nineteenth century were often using the repeating block format.

The contrast of the Midwestern block-style quilt with that of the Lancaster County medallion-style quilt suggests that the two traditions developed separately. The fact that many of the major Midwestern Amish settlements were founded before the advent of prolific Amish quiltmaking supports this premise.[12] Eve Wheatcroft Granick notes that there are "only a handful of quilts which are dated or accurately traced" to the 1850s, 1860s, and 1870s.[13] Evidence from probate records and dated Amish quilts suggests that the Amish did not start making quilts with any frequency until the last quarter of the nineteenth century. The earliest existing, dated Amish quilt is embroidered with the date 1849.[14] Quilts began appearing in Amish family inventories earlier in the Ohio settlements than in Lancaster County.[15] This evidence might help explain the two distinct traditions.

It is possible that Amish quiltmakers in both the Midwestern and Lancaster County styles began making quilts relatively late in comparison to mainstream American quiltmakers. This may have been due to the tumultuous period in Amish history which led eventually to the schism between the Old Order and Amish-Mennonite groups. Rather than just one schism occurring at a specific date, divisions occurred at different times in various geographic settlements.[16] Historian Theron Schlabach uses 1865 as a rough date for the emergence of the Old Order Amish as a distinct group. After that point, the Amish bishops and ministers who were cautious about change stopped attending the

(continued on page 33)

Figure 3

Advertisement placed in *The Sugarcreek Budget*, 1907, by a land agent in Ford County, Kansas. Advertisements such as this one enticed Amish members to move west in search of good land and economic prosperity.

Plate 23
Stars
Maker unknown • 1910-1930 • Possibly made in Kalona, Iowa • 33.5" x 28"
Wools, cottons • QSPI: 7-9
International Quilt Study Center, Sara Miller Collection, 2000.007.0069

This maker pieced her quilt in the classic Midwestern format with blocks arranged on point and separated by setting squares. Although the maker followed a standard design scheme, improvisation is also evident: most of the stars are pieced with a black background, but two have a dark green background instead. Each of the tiny triangles used to piece the stars has a leg of only ¾". The quiltmaker ran out of matching greens in one star and used three different shades to complete it.

Plate 24
One Patch
Maker unknown • 1900-1920 • Possibly made in Kalona, Iowa • 32.5" x 29.5"
Cottons • QSPI: 6-8
International Quilt Study Center, Sara Miller Collection, 2000.007.0080

The squares in this One Patch quilt are set on point, or diagonally, and framed by a narrow black frame and a wider brown border. Brown fabric is more common to nineteenth century and early twentieth century Amish quilts, as are the curved corners of the bound quilt edge.

Plate 25
Bear's Paw
Maker unknown • 1900-1920 • Probably made in Holmes County, Ohio • 45" x 36"
Cottons • QSPI: 7-9
International Quilt Study Center, Sara Miller Collection, 2000.007.0008

This Bear's Paw quilt shows many classic elements of Midwestern Amish quilt design. The field consists of repeating pieced blocks in a variety of muted, solid colors, each oriented on point (diagonally) with a setting square separating the pieced blocks. A narrow frame separates the field from the wide outer border. Black was a favored background color, particularly in the Ohio Amish settlements.

annual meetings which had aimed to resolve differences between the two groups.[17]

The genesis of Amish quiltmaking coincided with the emergence of the Old Order Amish following those years of struggle between the more conservative and the more progressive Amish factions.[18] The more tradition-minded Amish saw a renewed need for a uniform and fixed *Ordnung*, including a strict prohibition against gaily colored or printed clothing.[19] Just as Amish dress practices served as a means of community boundary maintenance for members of the Amish church, so could a distinct quilting style symbolically remind members of their renewed desire to be separate from the modernizing world. Perhaps Amish women developed the Amish quilt style as a further statement of their desire to be distinctly separate from "the world." Automobiles, tractors, and telephones hadn't yet entered the symbolic lexicon of either mainstream society or those living in resistance to it. Plain, dark-colored quilts with unprinted fabrics could have been a symbolic way for the Old Order Amish to take a different path when intersecting with the ornamental, consumer-oriented world of Victorian America and with their Amish-Mennonite cousins who were more ready to embrace some modern practices.

Through the 1930s, the Midwestern Amish used primarily dark, solid-colored fabrics, which originally characterized all Amish quilts. They did, however, often work with cotton, rather than wool, the preferred choice in Lancaster County. In contrast to a typical Lancaster Amish quilt, a classic Midwestern Amish quilt is pieced in a block format, often with the blocks set on point (in a diagonal orientation) with unpieced setting squares separating the pieced blocks, like the quilts shown in Plates 25 and 26.

Some lighter colored quilts featuring whites or pastels (see Plates 27 and 28) also were created by Midwestern Amish women, particularly in communities further west, which often had more lax interpretations of the *Ordnung*. Sara Miller refers to these quilts as "summer quilts" and does not seem at all surprised by the use of lighter colors. Lighter colored quilts may, in fact, have been much more common than quilt collectors and enthusiasts care to believe. They are not as

Plate 26
Lost Ships
Maker unknown
1900-1920
Possibly made in Haven, Kansas
43.5" x 36"
Cottons
QSPI: 6-8
International Quilt Study Center,
Sara Miller Collection, 2000.007.0054

Many Kansas Amish quiltmakers remained influenced by the quiltmaking practices of their "mother" communities in northern Indiana, from where many Kansas Amish migrated. In both Kansas and Indiana, quiltmakers often used red in quilts. The color was not a permissible choice for dresses, but was frequently purchased specifically for use in quilts, according to Eve Wheatcroft Granick in *The Amish Quilt*.

Plate 27
Stars
Mrs. Lizzie Miller • 1930-1950 • Probably made in Holmes County, Ohio • 46.5" x 31.5"
Cottons • QSPI: 6-7
International Quilt Study Center, Sara Miller Collection, 2000.007.0002

Sara Miller refers to light colored quilts such as this one as "summer quilts." The repeating block pattern, the use of a wide outer border and narrow inner frame, and the quilting designs all reflect typical Midwestern Amish quilting practices. The pastel color palette, however, contradicts our usual expectation of Amish quilts.

distinctly "Amish" in appearance and therefore have less appeal to "English" collectors.

Many of the quilts in the Miller Collection suggest that the smaller format provided by the crib quilt gave Amish quiltmakers the opportunity to experiment and expand the boundaries of the guidelines that silently governed Amish quiltmaking. Bettina Havig likens this freedom to contemporary quiltmakers who try more innovative designs on a small wallhanging piece rather than on a full-size quilt.[20] Some of the most improvisational pieces in this collection are adapted from traditional quilt designs, whether from the Lancaster County tradition or from mainstream American quiltmaking.

The quilt in Plate 29 is an example of this sort of innovation. The traditional Center Diamond (as seen in Figure 4), one of the most common Lancaster County quilt patterns, is found hidden in the Pine Tree quilt from Arthur, Illinois. The black field on which the tree rests is the center diamond, with the blue and red forming the traditional frames around the diamond. Like the Lancaster County quilts in the Center Diamond format, this quilt also has square dimensions in contrast to the more typical rectangular format used in the Midwest. The Pine Tree, however, is not a traditional Amish pattern (see Figure 5, "English" Pine Tree quilt). Historically the Amish refrained from using such representational images in their quilt designs. This quiltmaker adapted an "English" design and placed it in a traditional Amish setting. While the Pine Tree block is usually repeated in a block pattern when used on a full-size quilt, this crib quilt features a single tree as its central motif. This Midwestern Amish quiltmaker was clearly aware of both mainstream and Lancaster County quiltmaking practices.

A key component of many Amish quilts is the use of multiple borders to frame the design field. Typical use of borders is found in the quilt shown in Plate 30, with a narrow contrasting frame separating the design field from a wider outer border. Simple frames are also featured on Plain quilts that have no pieced central design, such as in those in Plates 31, 32, 33, and 34. Some scholars have suggested that these borders and frames in quilts may mirror the deliberate boundaries the Amish place on their lives through the *Ordnung*.[21]

(continued on page 41)

Plate 28
Baskets
Maker unknown
1930-1950
Made in Midwestern United States
42.5" x 35"
Cottons
QSPI: 8-10
International Quilt Study Center,
Sara Miller Collection, 2000.007.0010

Amish quilting trends generally lagged several decades behind those of mainstream American quiltmakers. Quilts featuring pastel "Easter egg" colors were popular with the general public from the 1910s through the 1930s. This quilt was likely made slightly later than this peak period when some Amish adopted limited use of these lighter colors. Whites and pastels in Amish quilts became more widespread in the 1940s, thus appropriately lagging behind the fashions of the "world."

Plate 29
Pine Tree
Maker unknown • 1900-1920 • Possibly made in Arthur, Illinois • 36.5" x 34"
Cottons, wool/cotton mixtures • QSPI: 6-7
International Quilt Study Center, Sara Miller Collection, 2000.007.0085

A striking Pine Tree motif is placed in a Center Diamond setting in this quilt (see Figure 4). The black field in which the tree rests is the center diamond, while blue and red form the traditional frames. The quiltmaker adapted this "English" representational design and placed it in a traditional Amish setting.

Figure 4
Center Diamond
Maker unknown, initialed "E.E."
Probably made in Lancaster County, Pennsylvania
1925-1945
81.5" x 80.5"
Top: rayon/acetate mixture (purple), wools;
    binding: rayon
QSPI: 9-10
International Quilt Study Center,
Ardis and Robert James Collection, 1997.007.0627

The Center Diamond is an example of the Lancaster County Amish medallion-style quilt featuring large color fields, which showcase intricate quilting designs.

Figure 5
Pine Tree
Maker unknown (Hutchins family)
Probably made in Indiana, Pennsylvania
1860-1880
69" x 69"
Cottons
QSPI: 9
International Quilt Study Center,
Ardis and Robert James Collection, 1997.007.0408

This quilt is an example of the Pine Tree pattern as made by a nineteenth-century "English" quiltmaker. Notice how the maker of the quilt in Plate 29 adapted the pattern and placed it in an Amish format.

Plate 30
Sixteen Patch
Maker unknown • 1900-1920 • Possibly made in Kalona, Iowa • 38" x 28.5"
Cottons • QSPI: 7-8
International Quilt Study Center, Sara Miller Collection, 2000.007.0018

Several different chambray fabrics are used in the piecing of this Sixteen Patch quilt. Chambray, a plain weave cloth woven with colored warp yarns and white weft yarns, has a soft heathered look. Amish women often used chambray to make their dresses, aprons, and children's clothing. According to Eve Wheatcroft Granick, Amish women also have used chambray to back quilts since the nineteenth century.

Plate 31
Plain Quilt
Maker unknown
1910-1930
Probably made in Indiana
36" x 33"
Wool (blue), cotton (yellow); back: cotton
QSPI: 7
International Quilt Study Center,
Sara Miller Collection, 2000.007.0077

The golden yellow double frame of this Plain quilt contrasts sharply with its deep blue ground. Yellow, one of the rarer hues found in Amish quilts, does not often appear in quilts of the Lancaster County Amish. The Indiana Amish, however, had a particular affinity for yellows, oranges, and bright reds, which were not often used for clothing, but may have been purchased expressly for quiltmaking.

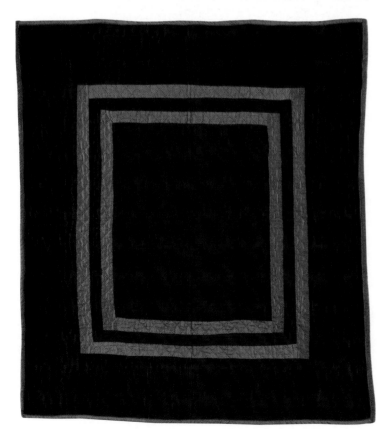

Plate 32
Plain Quilt
Maker unknown
1920-1940
Probably made in Wayne County, Ohio
34.5" x 31"
Cottons
QSPI: 6
International Quilt Study Center,
Sara Miller Collection, 2000.007.0026

The simple arrangement of this pristine double-framed Plain quilt is characteristic of the full-size Plain quilts commonly made in the Amish communities of eastern Ohio. The use of rich cotton sateen fabric makes the solid black ground look anything but "plain." Subtly emerging from the rich black field are a quilted feathered wreath, eight-pointed star, and fan arcs, all complimented by a 3/4"-square grid. The wine-colored sateen used in the frames breaks up the black ground and is repeated in the quilt's binding.

Plate 33
Plain Quilt
Mrs. Menno Schlabach
1930-1950
Probably made in Wayne County, Ohio
34" x 28.5"
Cottons
QSPI: 8-10
International Quilt Study Center,
Sara Miller Collection, 2000.007.0017

This quilt is another fine example of the Amish Plain quilt. Plain quilts continued to be made with some frequency as crib quilts after they were seldom made as full-size quilts, perhaps because a top could be completed with a small amount of fabric. With a mere yard of fabric, an adequate Plain crib quilt could be assembled quite readily.

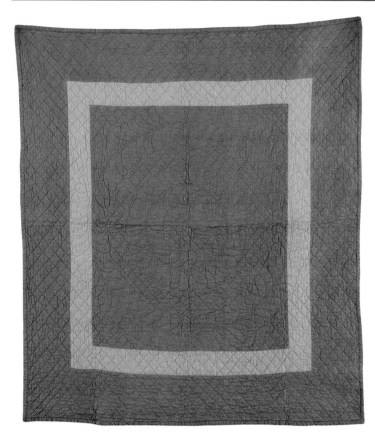

Plate 34
Plain Quilt
Maker unknown
1930-1950
Possibly made in Independence, Iowa
37" x 33"
Cottons
QSPI: 7-8
International Quilt Study Center,
Sara Miller Collection, 2000.007.0048

Plain quilts, similar to this one, were likely among the earliest made by the Amish. As with the "English" whole cloth quilt, the expanse of unpieced cloth often served as a canvas for intricate quilting designs. The interior field of this quilt features a double feathered wreath framing a grid of fine quilting stitches.

Some crib quiltmakers exploited this quiltmaking practice by adapting the typical use of frames and borders into a new design scheme. An extreme example is found in Plate 35. The design field is shrunk to feature only one pieced star measuring nine inches. Five borders surround the star, elevating the framing device from a secondary design feature to a primary motif. In Plate 36, narrow frames are superimposed over a checkerboard field, creating an illusion of depth. In an adaptation of the simple Plain pattern, the quilt in Plate 37 features dark frames surrounding two red squares. Again, the framing borders are the most prominent feature of the design, rather than a typical pieced block design.

American Fascination with Amish Culture

The American fascination with Amish quilts is an indication of Americans' tendency to romanticize a culture that is deemed exotic, in this case the perceived simplified lifestyle led by the Old Order Amish, surrounded by the hectic pace of modern society. Unlike mysteriously intriguing cultures far from North Amer-

ica, the Amish are appealing in part because they represent America's past. Sociologist Marc Olshan suspects that "One reason for our attraction to the Amish is that we miss at least part of what we suspect we have lost."[22]

Amish quilts are a recognizable manifestation of this cultural group. In recent decades, Amish quilts have captivated a broad audience. Amish quilts first received widespread public attention during Jonathan Holstein and Gail van der Hoof's 1971 landmark exhibition, "Abstract Design in American Quilts" at the Whitney Museum of American Art. Holstein was initially attracted to Amish quilts for their similarity to modern art, such as Albers' *Homage to the Square*.[23] Upon seeing this exhibition, soon-to-be collectors Faith and Stephen Brown were also "profoundly moved by the graphic power" of Amish quilts.[24] Likely, these early collectors were intrigued by the dichotomy of something they viewed as so modern emerging out of a culture appearing so old-fashioned. Art critic Robert Hughes hypothesizes that Amish quilts are set apart from many other forms of folk art because they look "inescapably modern. . . .

(continued on page 47)

Plate 35
Star
Mrs. Miller
1920-1940
Probably made in Holmes County, Ohio
38.5" x 37.5"
Cottons
QSPI: 7-8
International Quilt Study Center,
Sara Miller Collection, 2000.007.0070

Borders are often an important design element in Amish quilts. This quiltmaker took the use of borders to the extreme by framing the nine-inch pieced star with five concentric borders. In doing so, the framing device was elevated from a secondary design element to a more prominent feature of the quilt.

41

Plate 36
One Patch variation
Maker unknown • 1920-1940 • Possibly made in Holmes County, Ohio • 32" x 30"
Cottons • QSPI: 7-8
International Quilt Study Center, Sara Miller Collection, 2000.007.0066

Narrow frames, typically used to surround the central design field in Midwestern Amish quilts, are instead here superimposed over a checkerboard field, creating an illusion of depth. An outer border of rich wine-colored cotton sateen frames the entire field, giving this quilt a warm glow.

Plate 37
Framed Squares
Maker unknown • 1900-1920 • Possibly made in Holmes County, Ohio • 51" x 34.5"
Wool/cotton mixtures, cottons • QSPI: 7
International Quilt Study Center, Sara Miller Collection, 2000.007.0023

Reminiscent of a nineteenth-century Lancaster County Amish quilt design known as Center Square, this quilt's beauty is in its simplicity. The two framed squares give the quilt the appearance of a paned window. The quiltmaker combined the rich red and purple twills of wool and cotton mixtures with a black cotton twill to form this striking design.

Plate 38
Nine Patch
Maker unknown • 1900-1920 • Possibly made in Arthur, Illinois • 40.5" x 33.5"
Top: wools, wool/cotton mixtures; back: cotton • QSPI: 7-8
International Quilt Study Center, Sara Miller Collection, 2000.007.0045

The Amish near Arthur, Illinois, may have used wool to piece quilts more often than was done in other Midwestern Amish settlements. Janice Tauer Wass, curator of "Illinois Amish Quilts: Sharing Threads of Tradition," at the Illinois State Museum, suggests that this is due, in part, to the presence of 11 woolen mills in close proximity to the Arthur settlement. The randomly pieced Nine Patch blocks in this quilt display this access to fine, richly colored wools.

Plate 39
Square in a Square
Maker unknown • 1910-1930 • Possibly made in Michigan • 45" x 34"
Wools, cottons • QSPI: 6-7
International Quilt Study Center, Sara Miller Collection, 2000.007.0049

The geometric pattern of the Square in a Square leaps off this quilt, due to the sharp contrast between the light yellow cotton pieces and the wools forming the navy ground, purple border, and black binding. This dramatic contrast in value fills this simple pattern with energy and movement.

45

Plate 40
Bow Tie
Maker unknown • 1920-1940 • Made in Midwestern United States; acquired in Clark, Missouri
47.5" x 34.5" • Cottons • QSPI: 7-8
International Quilt Study Center, Sara Miller Collection, 2000.007.0061

   This quiltmaker's placement of Bow Tie blocks results in the appearance of gray circles floating on top of the quilt's surface. Bow Tie is a pattern that was popular among "English" quiltmakers and adopted by their Amish neighbors.

AMISH SCHOOL CHILDREN OF LANCASTER COUNTY, PA.

Figure 6

This postcard with caption reading, "Amish School Children of Lancaster County, Pa," features a photograph from around the beginning of the twentieth century. The date of publication for this postcard is unknown, but it is an early example of a souvenir available to tourists visiting Pennsylvania's "Amish Country."
Image courtesy of the Mennonite Historical Library, Goshen, Indiana.

But that is an illusion: the truth is that Amish quilts embody the reductionism, the search for fundamentals, that modernism wanted to find in more 'primitive' cultures. . . . In fact, they come from a culture to which modernism is anathema."[25]

American fascination with the Amish did not begin during the genesis of the current quilt revival in the 1970s. Starting in the 1930s, the "Pennsylvania Dutch" country of eastern Pennsylvania surrounding the Lancaster County Amish settlement was promoted in tourism literature.[26] With the opening of the Pennsylvania Turnpike in the early 1940s, this region was easily accessed by tourists looking for an escape from the hustle and bustle of East Coast cities.[27] If this desire to retreat to a quieter, simpler world was apparent in the 1940s, it has only intensified in tandem with the increasingly hectic pace of society. In subsequent decades, the presence of tourism similarly became a

Figure 7

This postcard, printed circa 1960, was likely one of the first postcards featuring Indiana's "Amish Country." The caption on the reverse reads, "Amish farmers threshing grain at harvest time. A familiar scene in Northern Indiana, moving from farm to farm, threshing becomes a community project."
Image courtesy of the Mennonite Historical Library, Goshen, Indiana. Photo by John Penrod, used with permission from Penrod/Hiawatha.

Plate 41
Hens and Chickens
Maker unknown • 1920-1940 • Made in Midwestern United States • 36" x 33"
Cottons • QSPI: 8-9
International Quilt Study Center, Sara Miller Collection, 2000.007.0044

Quilt pattern names such as "Hens and Chickens" are evocative of the rural, agrarian lifestyle the Amish have historically lived. Other patterns found in the Miller Collection with names reminiscent of farm life include Hole in the Barn Door, Rail Fence, and Straight Furrow. Despite the large numbers of Amish no longer farming, such names will likely continue to be used for both Amish and "English" quilts, because they evoke images of an often romanticized simpler past.

This quilt was acquired in Kalona, Iowa, the long-time home of Sara Miller. Sara moved with her family to Iowa as a young woman, after growing up in Kokomo, Indiana. Sara speaks with special fondness of quilts like this one which were "made local." The practice of using lighter colors, such as the blues and pinks found in this quilt, began earlier in the Kalona area than in other Midwestern Amish settlements.

reality in Amish settlements from Ohio westward.[28] In the 1950s, following the comedic portrayal of the Amish in the successful Broadway musical, *Plain and Fancy,* American fascination with the Amish was, according to author David Weaver-Zercher, largely based on "the nostalgic desire to revisit the simple life of America's past."[29] He also notes the irony that in the process of searching for the simplicity the Amish represent, tourists and others participated in mass consumerism of anything representative of the Amish culture, including quilts.[30]

Tourists visiting Amish country sought out quilts as souvenirs of their trip to this quieter world. As antique Amish quilts increased in popularity, so did the prices collectors were willing to pay for old quilts. At the same time, the Amish adapted their quiltmaking practices again, this time using popular nontraditional designs which appealed to certain segments of the tourist market.[31] In this sense, the collision of tourism with Amish culture was not a simple one-way street in which tourists drove by and gawked at the Amish.

Today the Amish participate economically in the tourism, quiltmaking, and quilt-collecting industries.

Their rapid population growth, the uncertainty of the farm economy, and the increased price of farmland have led to an increased rate of Amish abandoning their agricultural occupations in favor of paid work elsewhere.[32] Home-based shops that sell to visitors are one such outlet.[33] Some shops, such as the one Sara Miller formerly owned, sell quilts made by Amish women on consignment. Other businesses specialize in made-to-order quilts.[34]

Like all successful entrepreneurs, Amish women making quilts for sale learn to know what their target customers want. In recent decades, many Amish quiltmakers, like their "English" counterparts, have utilized synthetic fabrics and puffy polyester batting to make quilts.

As the popularity of antique Amish quilts increased, some contemporary Amish quiltmakers have instead attempted to imitate the highly sought after antique quilts. A crib quilt in the Amish and Mennonite Museum Collection at Goshen (Indiana) College illustrates this. The quilt, pieced from cotton in traditional muted colors, resembles many of the quilts found in the Miller Collection. It, however, is not an antique. Collection records indicate that the young Amish quilt-

Plate 43
Nine Patch
Maker unknown • 1920-1940 • Possibly made in Ohio; acquired in Missouri • 33" x 24"
Cottons • QSPI: 10-11
International Quilt Study Center, Sara Miller Collection, 2000.007.0012

This light colored quilt has a feature popular among Ohio Amish and Mennonite quiltmakers during the 1920s and 1930s: a style of binding which serves a purpose beyond mere utility. Referred to as "sawtooth binding," this method creates a decorative repeating triangle design at the edge of the quilt. The technique may have been a special finish that quiltmakers requested from particularly skilled needlewomen.

maker made the quilt with the intention of selling it only after she had used and washed it for several years to give it a softly worn look, just as if it had been made in the early twentieth century. Her entrepreneurial approach paid off: auction records reveal that this quiltmaker was able to sell her quilt for considerably more than her sister received for her unfaded, polyester-filled quilt.[35]

Intersecting With One's Own Culture: Sara Miller's Story

The Miller Collection of Amish crib quilts was collected by Sara Miller of Kalona, Iowa, from the mid-1980s through the late 1990s. Unlike most other major collectors of Amish quilts, Miller spent most of her life as a member of the Amish church. Sara has the unique experience of being an Amish insider who interacted with the outside world through her collection of Amish quilts. She grew up in Kokomo, Indiana, and moved with her parents as a young adult to the Amish settlement in Kalona.

As a young person, she thought that traditional Amish quilts in dark, plain colors were "extremely ugly." She would have preferred to receive store-bought bedspreads rather than the typical quilts "from home" that Amish young adults receive from their mothers. Her mother compromised and gave her quilts featuring lighter colors, similar to the lighter-colored quilts that eventually became part of her own collection (see Plates 43 and 44).

After her parents died in the late 1970s, Miller began to think about the old family quilts. The quilts her grandmothers made had been largely used up during the Depression, although Miller knew a few were used later for packing. Miller serendipitously discovered one of these old packing quilts in her woodhouse. This particular quilt had a top which her mother had pieced and an old used quilt as its filler. Miller describes her find:[36]

> Curiosity got the best of me. I snipped a little away, opened a little, and saw what was very beautiful quilting. So that evening after work—I couldn't hardly wait until after work—I sat down on the liv-

Plate 44
Log Cabin, Straight Furrow variation
Maker unknown
1930-1950
Made in Midwestern United States
56" x 39"
Cottons
QSPI: 8
International Quilt Study Center,
Sara Miller Collection, 2000.007.0022

Unlike most quilts in the Miller Collection, this quilt shows clear signs of heavy use. Stains and tears from unknown sources suggest that this quilt may have many stories to tell. Visible in one abraded area is a cotton blanket, used as the batting of the quilt.

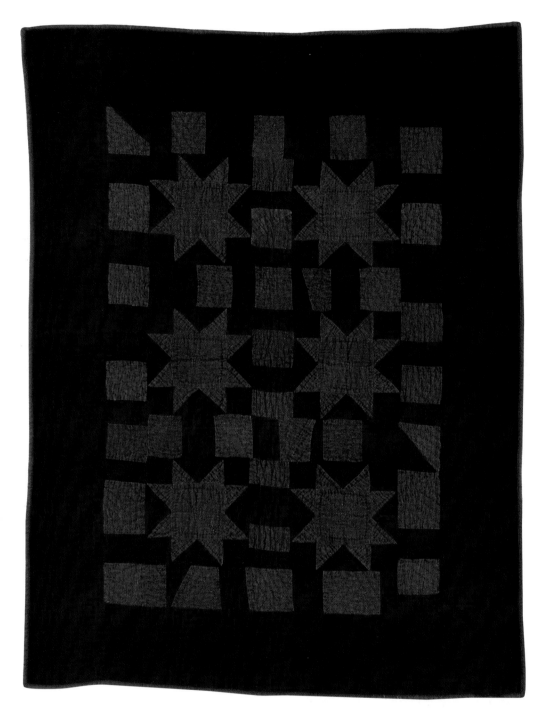

Plate 45
Stars
Maker unknown • 1900-1920 • Possibly made in Independence, Iowa • 36" x 28"
Cottons • QSPI: 6-7
International Quilt Study Center, Sara Miller Collection, 2000.007.0029

Black and dark blue are both popular color choices in Midwestern Amish quilts. The combination of the two colors, however, creates a quilt with very low contrast between foreground and background. A close look reveals that the six stars are set between sashing that is pieced of black and blue irregular shapes.

ing room floor and carefully opened it all up. Of course the original quilt was just in shambles, but it had beautiful quilting. I began to wonder if this was maybe something one of my grandmothers had made. I thought I'd have to ask an aunt . . . But I didn't need to. Because the next morning I hung it out on the line. I actually sponged it very carefully, because it was filthy dirty. And right in the center of the quilt my grandmother had quilted my dad's initials and the year. So I knew it was one that my grandmother had made.

I recreated it later. I made one out of cotton sateen . . . and it has crisscross with feathers [quilting], and then wonderful feather [quilting] designs and other [quilting] designs, too. And that got me really wondering about quilts and patterns, and so one day I just said out of the blue, "Someday I wanna own one."

Around this same time, Miller learned of "English people coming from Chicago and places . . . how they liked the old Amish quilts."[37] The fascination of these outsiders with Amish quilts spurred Miller's own growing interest in Amish quilts. Occasionally someone would bring an old Amish quilt in to sell at Miller's shop, Kountry Kreations. Her own interest developed to the point that:

One day, this fellow who dealt [in quilts]. . . brought me one in, and I said, "That's it". . . it was

a local Kalona quilt. And so I bought that one. Well, I've often said it's kind of like trying to eat one Frito. So I bought more from him![38]

So began this unusual relationship of an Amish woman to Amish quilts. Unlike collectors initially attracted to the intense colors and bold graphics of Amish quilts, Miller had to learn to appreciate the dark palette she once viewed as dull. She first liked Amish quilts because they brought her closer to her own heritage. She speaks of the quiltmakers as "mothers" and of her amazement at the many babies who slept under these small quilts. Sara relates in a personal way to the quilts in this collection—something not entirely possible for collectors outside the Amish culture.

Miller's own quiltmaking practices changed as her interest in old Amish quilts grew. Her new appreciation for the older quilts helped her to embrace the more traditional quiltmaking practices common during her youth. She had adopted the mainstream quiltmaking practices of the 1970s and 1980s. She describes this series of changes:

On fabrics, you know, we thought it was so wonderful when you could get the polyester cotton [blends]. Now, I'm a cotton person, or wool . . . I went through a whole reformation . . . also in quilting; I like lots of quilting now. When polyester batting first came out, we thought the puffier the bet-

Figure 8

Sara Miller owned and operated the fabric and craft consignment shop, Kountry Kreations, for over 20 years. The shop was located in the barn on her farm in the country outside Kalona, Iowa.

Plate 46
Stars
Maker unknown • 1920-1940 • Possibly made in Haven, Kansas • 35" x 29"
Cottons • QSPI: 8
International Quilt Study Center, Sara Miller Collection, 2000.007.0032

Several details make this quilt particularly unusual. The quiltmaker used not one, but three, narrow frames to set off the design field, in addition to a wide border. Each star is contained within a four-inch square and is pieced with four obtuse triangles added to the central square to form the star. Tiny equilateral triangles were added to create eight points on each star.

Plate 47
Log Cabin, Straight Furrow variation
Maker unknown
1930-1950
Possibly made in Indiana
41" x 32"
Cottons, wool/cotton mixtures
QSPI: 7
International Quilt Study Center,
Sara Miller Collection, 2000.007.0027

With no knowledge of color theory, this quiltmaker used predominantly cool-color fabrics—blues, greens, and purples—to piece the straight furrows in this Log Cabin quilt. One deep-red hearth square provides contrast to the primarily cool colors found throughout. Careful examination shows the use of a wide variety of fabric weaves.

---

ter. You didn't have to quilt as much. Now I'm just the other way; I like lots of quilting.[39]

Collecting from one's own culture may in some ways be more challenging than collecting from an exoticized culture of the "other." Miller struggled internally with the commodification of Amish quilts. She did not want to haggle over a proposed price; she preferred to tell her dealer simply "yes" or "no." Miller's primary dealer went door-to-door in Amish communities hunting for quilts. Miller described feeling guilty about benefiting from his tactics: "I felt bad; I have felt bad about that through the years, because I know some of them he got off of people who did not want to sell 'em."

She says that she never would have considered going door-to-door herself; perhaps this sort of forthright strategy ran too counter to her Amish sense of humility. But others benefited from his door-to-door strategy. Miller recounted how many Amish and formerly Amish individuals had little trouble parting with their old dark quilts. Those who initially were reluctant to

sell sometimes changed their mind when they needed quick money for a specific cause, such as surgery.[40]

Miller's dealer often withheld information from her about who made a quilt. She suspects that he was trying to protect his business and did not want to enable Miller to contact the families herself. This, too, often frustrated Miller. The larger Amish community is highly interconnected, so that individuals often are acquainted with, if not related to, persons in settlements several states away. Extensive migration from settlement to settlement and the practices of Amish intermarriage contribute to "everyone knowing everyone else." Miller often racked her brain to figure out who may have made quilts that her dealer said he bought in the Kalona area. Miller describes how she deduced who made one particular quilt in her private collection:[41]

And when he brought this one in, he kind of made a slip of the tongue, and he said, "I bought this in Charm, Ohio, on a high hill." And I didn't think about it until after he had left and I thought,

Plate 48
Herringbone
Maker unknown • 1910-1930 • Possibly made in Holmes County Ohio • 45" x 33.5"
Wools, wool/cotton mixtures, cottons • QSPI: 5-6
International Quilt Study Center, Sara Miller Collection, 2000.007.0006

The maker pieced individual strips of dress-weight fabrics at angles, creating an illusion of depth in this Herringbone pattern. Sara Miller, who owned and operated a successful fabric store for years, thinks this arrangement looks like stacked-up bolts of fabric.

"I know where you bought that."... Because these people lived on a high hill. And the woman, I'm just positive, that her mother probably made this for [her]. She was an only child. And her dad was my mother's first cousin. So you know, it's family. So the next time he came, I said, "You told me this quilt was from a high hill in Charm. I know where you bought that," and I named the people, and he didn't deny it. He just said, "There's more than one high hill." I'm just sure, you know, that that's where that little gem comes from.

Charm is just one small village populated by Amish and Mennonites in Holmes County in eastern Ohio. This story demonstrates Miller's intuitive knowledge of information that collectors from the outside would spend years trying to sort out. Miller's position as an Amish insider allowed her to intersect with her own culture through quilts, such as this "gem" from Charm.

Due, in part, to her active role as a quilt collector and her entrepreneurial position as the owner of a successful fabric shop, Miller's own life has also intersected with many cultures other than Amish. Admittedly, Sara Miller has not led the traditional life of an Amish woman whose primary role is usually mother and farmwife. As a collector, Miller often traveled with her small quilts to present lectures on Amish quiltmaking.

Her active participation in relief work through Christian Aid Ministries allowed her to piece quilts with a purpose. In one year she made over 100 quilt tops to send to Romania for relief. She also traveled to Romania as part of this service. When she retired from owning and running her fabric store, she sent close to 10,000 yards of her inventory to Romania. The fabric was used by community women whom she helped support through relief work in their sewing projects. Her position as businesswoman and world traveler would likely not have been possible if she had married, as the majority of Amish women do. She says that she is one of many unmarried Amish women in the Kalona area, where females outnumber males. But she is adamant that marriage was not meant for her, and that she would have missed many wonderful experiences if she had been tied down to a family. She also insists, however, that she missed many blessings for the same reason.

Miller clearly cherishes the variety of quilts represented in this collection. "I think that quilts have different points that appeal," she says, highlighting the crude workmanship on a simple One Patch quilt pictured in Plate 49. She also is drawn to quilts with a contemporary, experimental look to them, such as the skewed Log Cabin shown in Plate 50. She longs to know why the quiltmakers made the choices that they did:

Plate 49
One Patch
Mrs. Jacob Schlabach
1920-1940
Probably made in Kalona, Iowa
33" x 32"
Cottons
QSPI: 5
International Quilt Study Center,
Sara Miller Collection, 2000.007.0031

Large quilting stitches in coarse, blue pearl cotton thread hold together the layers of this simple One Patch quilt. Sara Miller hypothesizes that this quilt was quickly assembled by a mother or older sister because "she needed a quilt for that baby." This quilt contrasts dramatically with many of the more intricately pieced and quilted examples found in the Miller collection.

Plate 50
Log Cabin variation
Maker unknown • 1910-1930 • Possibly made in Indiana; acquired in Haven, Kansas
38" x 28" • Cottons, a bit of wool • QSPI: 6-7
International Quilt Study Center, Sara Miller Collection, 2000.007.0046

A dramatic departure from the typical Amish design sensibilities that emphasize restraint, simplicity, and order, this Log Cabin variation is pieced from irregular, skewed logs. A quilt from Indiana with a strikingly similar design is depicted in Eve Wheatcroft Granick's *The Amish Quilt* (page 156). This quilt was acquired in Haven, Kansas. Many young women from the Amish settlements in northern Indiana moved to Kansas as newly married women. Perhaps this quilt and the similar quilt from Indiana (in Granick's book) have a shared history originating in Indiana.

Plate 51
String Star
Maker unknown
1900-1920
Made in Midwestern United States
40" x 33.5"
Cottons
QSPI: 6-7
International Quilt Study Center,
Sara Miller Collection, 2000.007.0015

This quilt shows the tendency for Amish crib quilts to be pieced from a variety of fabrics. The blue border that frames the star is made from very loosely woven cotton with irregularly spun yarns. This cloth contrasts with the black twill cotton fabric used in the ground, and the fine cotton sateen used to back the quilt.

I think I could describe it better if I could talk to those mothers . . . a lot of them are no longer alive. But you know, to ask them. . .there are a lot of things I could have asked my mom about, but I wasn't interested. [If only] I could go back and say, "Now why did you do that?"

Miller realizes that this collection of crib quilts is unique because of its connection to her own Amish heritage:

It took me a long time to appreciate it, my heritage. It's like I often said, if I ever had made [quilts] in the tradition that I should [have], some of the quilts that I got from home would be valuable by now. But I think it has given me a deeper appreciation because it took me so long to see . . . Lots of girls get married young and they could care less about the older things, and I don't know . . . It's unusual, but I like unusual things, you know.

* * *

We can view the quilts in the Miller collection and develop interpretations based solely on our understanding of their stitches, colors, and patterns. And we can read them by placing them in their cultural context. But quilts, unfortunately, cannot speak back. Sara Miller bemoaned the fact that the individual stories of each quilt are unknowable: "As simple as it is, I think they all have stories, if you could just untangle [them]!"[42] We cannot know the names of all the children who slept under these quilts. We will never know why some of these quilts are in pristine, never-been-used condition, while others are faded and softly worn. These individual stories may indeed be lost. But the quilts do allow us to explore the culture in which they were made and used.

Like many aspects of Amish culture, Amish quiltmaking has not emerged, nor has it been maintained, in a vacuum. Both Amish culture and Amish quiltmaking have been continually evaluated, whether subconsciously or deliberately, by members within the

Plate 52
Nine Patch variation
Maker unknown • 1920-1940 • Possibly made in Arthur, Illinois • 37.5" x 30.5"
Cottons • QSPI: 6-7
International Quilt Study Center, Sara Miller Collection, 2000.007.0089

A single block of orange fabric jumps from the center of the top row of this quilt. This block contrasts with much of the design field, which the maker pieced from softly heathered blue, gray, purples, and red chambrays. A quilted 10-petal flower belies the simplicity of each Nine Patch variation block.

Plate 53
Ocean Waves
Mrs. J. A. Yoder
1910-1930
Probably made in Arthur, Illinois
38" x 30.5"
Cottons
QSPI: 5
International Quilt Study Center,
Sara Miller Collection, 2000.007.0068

The maker's innovative use of the Ocean Waves pattern results in a center medallion setting, rather than the block format typically used (see Plate 72) with this pattern. The sole Ocean Waves block in this quilt is pieced from triangles cut from an assortment of fabrics, rather than a deliberate pairing of one (or several) colors with black triangles, as is typically done. These small triangles are hand-pieced, while the longer seams are machine-pieced.

community. And Amish quilt patterns, techniques, and colors have changed and been adapted through the years. It is a romanticized notion to view the Amish or their quilts as purely products of another era. Amish quilts were and are made by women who struggle to lead lives within the boundaries of their communities' *Ordnung*. But these same women's lives have intersected with mainstream American society in numerous ways, some of which are reflected in their quilts. We who view these quilts intersect with Amish culture when we delight in the quilts' rich colors, innovative patterns, and charming scale. They are an entry point to a culture much different than, but often at a crossroads with, that of the larger world.

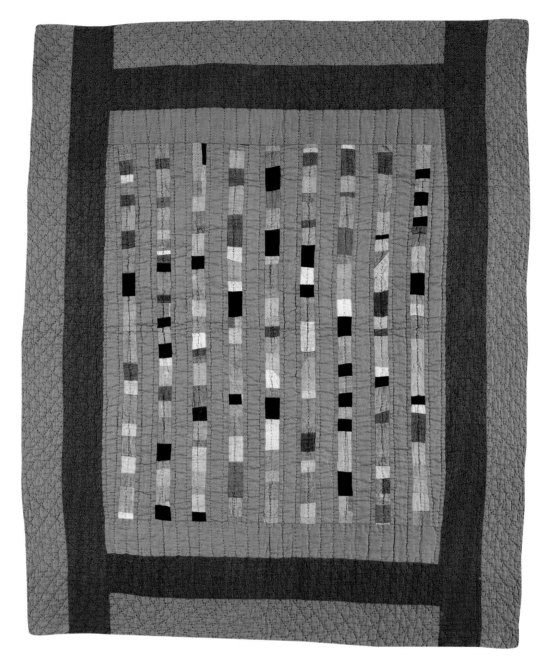

Plate 54
Chinese Coins
Maker unknown • 1920-1940 • Probably made in Arthur, Illinois • 37" x 31"
Cottons • QSPI: 7-8
International Quilt Study Center, Sara Miller Collection, 2000.007.0084

Quilts from this rather isolated Amish community are thought to exhibit a greater freedom of design than those from some other Amish communities. Scholars theorize that the Illinois location on the "frontier" enabled greater experimentation in quiltmaking styles, when compared with the more settled communities in Pennsylvania. For example, a significant number of distinctly Amish crazy quilts were made in Arthur. This Chinese Coins quilt reflects an unstructured "crazy" design preference. The strips of scraps resemble thin crazy quilts in the variety of angles and fabrics used. Unlike the exuberant crazy quilts of the Victorian Era, this quilt is muted by the soft colors used in the strips, and the gray and tan background fabrics.

SYMMETRY IN AMISH QUILTS

by Linda Welters

Amish quilts have long been admired for their distinctive visual qualities. Characterized by striking geometric patterns and somber hues, they command a unique place in the history of American quilts. Art historians and quilt scholars alike have interpreted them as abstract art.[1] Amish quilts may be appreciated without knowing who produced them. Yet in today's global society, the possibility of gaining insight into Amish culture through quilts adds to their mystique. In this essay, symmetry, one of the underlying principles of design, is applied to the Sara Miller Collection of Amish crib quilts to explore how art intersects with culture.

The fascination with Amish quilts is intensified by curiosity about the Amish themselves.[2] The Amish are a sectarian religious group who came to North America beginning in the 1730s and established themselves as farmers. They lived among, but separate from, other rural dwellers in the Pennsylvania counties in which they first settled. Throughout the nineteenth and twentieth centuries, the Amish formed new settlements in the East, the Midwest, and Ontario, Canada.[3]

The Amish emerged from the Anabaptist religious movement. The Amish community is structured around the attitude of *Gelassenheit*, which literally means "submission."[4] It embodies the Amish values of obedience, humility, and simplicity. Amish persons' lives are governed by the *Ordnung*, a set of unwritten regulations which each congregation revises periodically.[5] This code of conduct includes guidelines for dress and appearance and, to a lesser degree, for appropriate fabrics and styles for quiltmaking. Both *Gelassenheit* and *Ordnung* discourage "prideful" behavior.

Authorities agree that Amish women learned quilting in the New World from their neighbors, whom they called the "English."[6] In Pennsylvania, these neighbors were other German immigrants and Quakers. In the Midwestern communities, the ethnic backgrounds of the "English" were much more diverse. Evidence from probate records reveals a preference among the Amish for coverlets, blankets, and other woven bed coverings before the last quarter of the nineteenth century.[7] Although quilts are listed in Amish estate inventories as early as 1831, the oldest extant quilt with an Amish provenance is dated 1849. The Amish seem to have adopted quilting rather late. Only a few quilts dated prior to 1870 are known. The bulk of Amish quilts in museum collections date from 1880 to 1960.

Early Amish quilt patterns are based on the whole cloth, medallion, and strip styles popular among American quiltmakers in the late eighteenth and early nineteenth centuries. Amish women also adopted the simple repeating block patterns that had replaced the medallion format by the 1840s among mainstream American quiltmakers.[8] Four Patch and Nine Patch proved to be particular favorites. Eventually Amish women added more complex blocks, such as Log Cabin, Basket, and Ocean Waves, to their repertoire of acceptable patterns. Scholars believe that the Amish deliberately chose conservative, old-fashioned patterns for their quilts.[9] In selecting colors, Amish women limited themselves to the same dark, solid-colored fabrics that they used for their clothing. As the twentieth century progressed, women in the various Amish communities scattered throughout the United States adopted a greater range of patterns and colors for their quilts.

Some distinctions exist between the designs of the Pennsylvania Amish and the Midwestern Amish.[10] While the Pennsylvania Amish are recognized for their large all-over patterns such as Center Diamond, Sunshine and Shadow, and Bars, the Midwestern Amish more often used repeating block patterns for their quilts. Corner blocks are characteristic of Pennsylvania Amish quilts; inner borders enclosing a pieced block field are common to Midwestern Amish quilts. Quilts made in the Pennsylvania communities use deep, saturated colors, while those from the more dispersed Midwestern congregations display a broader palette, particularly the greater use of black. Pennsylvania quilts are often square in shape, whereas Midwestern quilts are rectangular. Wool was the fiber of choice for Pennsylvania quilts, but cotton made its way into the Midwestern quilts. Exquisite quilting, often in elaborate patterns, can be found in all Amish quilts.

Although much has been written about Amish quilt design, no one has attempted a systematic evaluation of symmetry in Amish quilts. A handful of authors have briefly addressed symmetry when discussing Amish quilts. In reference to the Center Diamond pattern, Patsy and Myron Orlofsky observed that: "the placement of a central point around which a pattern is symmetrically arranged" is common to the medallion quilts, bed rugs, and Indian palampores so prevalent in the eighteenth century.[11] Amelia Peck of the Metropolitan Museum of Art echoes this observation.[12] Joe Cunningham commented on the range of symmetries he observed in Amish quilts, from the formal, strictly organized medallion and block formats to "rogue blocks" and random arrangements resulting from color variations and irregular-sized patches.[13]

Even fewer authors explore in detail how design elements in Amish quilts reflect their culture. Eve Granick's thorough work links variations in the Amish design repertoire to the communities that produced them, showing that Amish quilts are far from homogeneous.[14] Sara Laurel Holstein, in a material culture appraisal of a single Center Diamond quilt, discusses the visual impact of a diamond set on point, proposing that the precariously positioned diamond, although symmetrical and regular, reflects a "societal uncertainty" and "insecurity" that "lies at the heart of the culture."[15] Jonathan Holstein eloquently discusses the aesthetics of Amish quilts in *A Quiet Spirit: Amish Quilts From the Collection of Cindy Tietze & Stuart Hodosh.*[16] His detailed analysis incorporates the origins, development, and characteristics of Amish quilts in Pennsylvania and Midwestern communities, including size, fabrics, color, patterns, and quilting designs.

In this essay, I analyze the use of symmetry as evidenced in the Sara Miller Collection of 90 Amish crib quilts. The technique used is a formal structural analysis based on mathematical principles. Amish crib quilts mirror full-sized Amish quilts in pattern, color, technique, and material.[17] All, except one of the quilts, are believed to be from Midwestern Amish settlements.[18] As a group, the Sara Miller quilts offer the opportunity to determine cultural preferences for symmetry among Amish quiltmakers in Midwestern communities. Symmetry of color and pattern is an important component of the design of quilts, particularly Amish quilts. It contributes to our ability to recognize an Amish quilt.

Symmetry Analysis

Symmetry is a fundamental organizing principle in nature and art. *Webster's Unabridged Dictionary* defines symmetry as "similarity of form or arrangement on either side of a dividing line or plane."[19] In common usage, symmetry is understood to mean bilateral symmetry—mirror reflection of parts across a vertical axis in a finite whole. The human body exhibits bilateral symmetry. A second type of symmetry—radial symmetry—is commonly observed in nature. Equal parts rotate around a point. Snowflakes and the petals of a flower exhibit radial symmetry.

Symmetry analysis is a mathematically based tool to classify the organization of repeating designs. Based on geometry, mathematicians and crystallographers divide symmetry into three classes: point groups, line groups, and plane groups.[20] To be symmetrical, a motif (e.g., basic unit) must repeat itself at least once around a point, along a line, or in a plane. The basic unit of repetition is referred to as a *motif, shape,* or *figure.*[21] Repeating motifs are termed *designs.* When designs repeat along a line or in a plane, they are called patterns. Repeating patterns are either *one-dimensional* (e.g., border, band, strip, frieze) or *two-dimensional* (e.g., all-over pattern, plane, field). Motifs that exhibit symmetrical arrangements around a point, but do not repeat along a line or a plane, are termed *finite* designs. To clarify these definitions, consider a daisy design (Figure 9). Each petal is a *motif* or *shape* while the entire flower is a *design.* The daisy by itself is a *finite* design. Daisies that repeat in a chain form a *one-dimensional* pattern. If the daisies repeat in two directions, the arrangement is a *two-dimensional* pattern.

The process of analyzing symmetry involves classifying motifs according to their arrangements. Four motions produce repetition: *translation, reflection, glide reflection,* and *rotation.* Translation is the repetition of a motif along a line. Reflection occurs when a motif is reflected on either side of a line. The reflection may be either vertical or horizontal, or both. Glide reflection is defined as a translation followed by a reflection. Rotation occurs when a motif repeats around a point. Each of the three symmetry classes (point groups, line groups, and plane groups) has its own internationally accepted notation using combinations of letters and numbers to signify the motion producing the repetition.

Using a triangle motif, these four motions are illustrated in Figure 10. The single motif is asymmetrical, producing no symmetrical motion. The motif repeated along a straight line exhibits translation. Repeat-

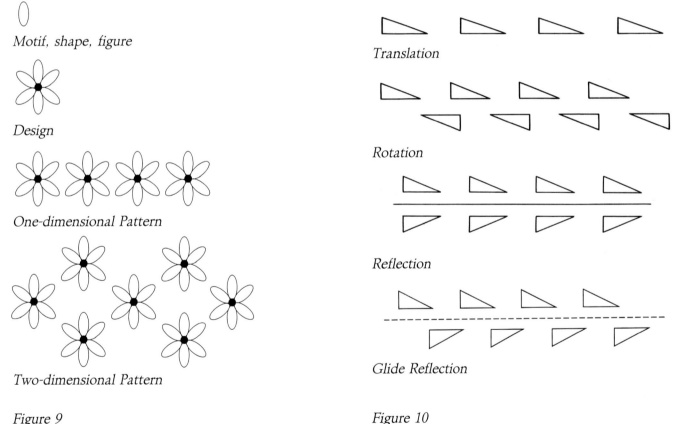

Motif, shape, figure

Design

One-dimensional Pattern

Two-dimensional Pattern

Translation

Rotation

Reflection

Glide Reflection

Figure 9

Illustrations of definitions for symmetry analysis: a single petal is a motif, shape, or figure; petals repeating around a center become a design; daisies in a row form a one-dimensional pattern; and daisies in an all-over arrangement create a two-dimensional pattern.

Figure 10

The four symmetry motions: translation, rotation, reflection, and glide reflection.

Adapted from Dorothy K. Washburn and Donald W. Crowe, *Symmetries of Culture: Theory and Practice of Plane Pattern Analysis* (Seattle: University of Washington Press, 1988). Reprinted by permission of the University of Washington Press.

ing the motif around a single point exhibits rotation. Reflection across a horizontal line, or a vertical line, or both, produces reflection symmetry. Repetition of the motif followed by reflection across a line admits glide reflection, like a human footprint.

The motions of symmetry may be found in all three classes of designs: finite, one-dimensional, and two-dimensional. Finite designs exhibit reflection and/or rotation but not translation or glide reflection (see Figure 11). (Finite designs that display rotation only carry the notation *c*, while those that both rotate and reflect are categorized as *d* designs.) An infinite number of finite designs are possible. Crystallographers have determined that only seven arrangements are possible for one-dimensional patterns. Figure 12 shows the seven one-dimensional patterns. Seventeen possible arrangements exist for two-dimensional patterns. Figure 13 shows the 17 two-dimensional patterns. When two colors are evenly distributed in a pattern, the possible arrangements expand to 46. Repetition of three-colored and four-colored patterns are theoretically possible but rare in reality.

Symmetry analysis is a useful tool to investigate the relationship between design and culture. It can be applied to repeating motifs in human-made objects such as tiles, pottery, basketry, woodcarvings, and textiles. At its most basic, symmetry analysis allows understanding of the organization of a pattern. When symmetries are compared across time and between cultures, symmetry analysis offers clues to group identity, contact between cultures, and expressions of belief systems.[22] Symmetry in nonrepresentational art may be interpreted as a metaphor for a culture's orientation to its world.[23] The metaphor is encoded in the way the shapes are structured in a whole pattern.

Studies of human perception show that across age groups and cultures, people react positively to symmetrical design. Infants as young as three and four months of age respond more actively to adults with well-balanced facial features.[24] Previous studies show that cultural groups limit themselves to a few preferred symmetries in their art.[25] Although members of a group may not know that they employ the same pattern arrangements in their art, the consistency of particular symmetries indicates that the selection of specific arrangements is not random.

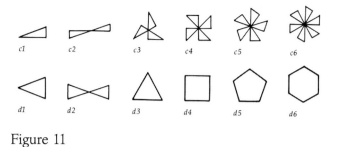

Figure 11

Finite designs (point groups).

Adapted from Dorothy K. Washburn and Donald W. Crowe, *Symmetries of Culture: Theory and Practice of Plane Pattern Analysis* (Seattle: University of Washington Press, 1988). Reprinted by permission of the University of Washington Press.

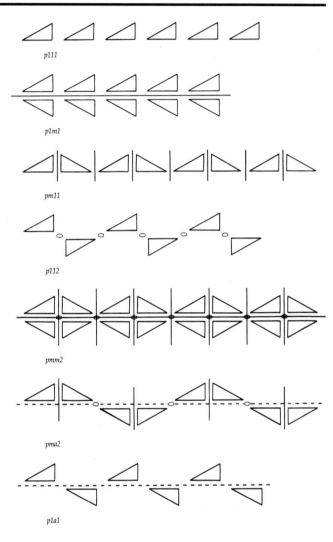

Figure 12

The seven one-dimensional patterns.

Adapted from Dorothy K. Washburn and Donald W. Crowe, *Symmetries of Culture: Theory and Practice of Plane Pattern Analysis* (Seattle: University of Washington Press, 1988). Reprinted by permission of the University of Washington Press.

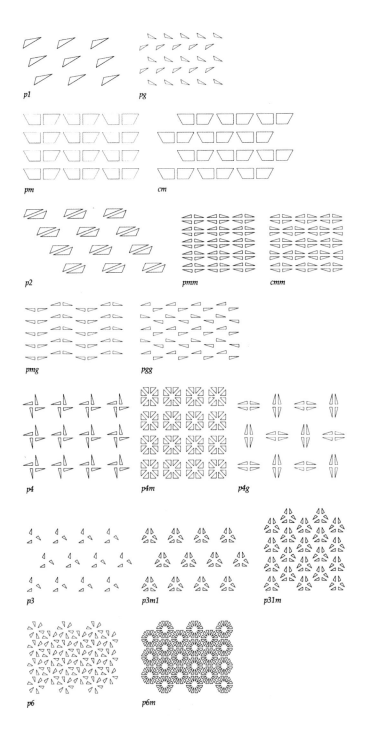

Figure 13

The 17 two-dimensional patterns.

Adapted from Dorothy K. Washburn and Donald W. Crowe, *Symmetries of Culture: Theory and Practice of Plane Pattern Analysis* (Seattle: University of Washington Press, 1988). Reprinted by permission of the University of Washington Press.

Studies of Symmetry in Textiles

A number of researchers have applied symmetry analysis to textiles. Carol Bier studied the symmetry of Oriental rugs, analyzing both border patterns and field patterns. She exhibited her findings at the Textile Museum in Washington, D.C. and published her results in a journal and on a website.[26] Researchers have studied symmetry in textiles of the highland Luzon in the Philippines, embroidered borders in Greek folk embroideries, Lithuanian patterned woven fabrics, and Thai textile patterns.[27] Although some of the work on symmetry in textiles emphasizes classification over interpretation, most studies conclude that each culture shows a decided preference for specific symmetries.

Symmetry in textiles can be traced to belief systems, as exemplified in a study of ikat fabrics from Sumba, Indonesia.[28] The preferred symmetries divided the surface into mirror images in three different fields, reflecting the organization of Sumbanese social groupings. They used the textiles in rituals, particularly burials, as indicators of rank and protection for the soul as it passed through to the other world.

Published studies on symmetry in quilts are rare, although the arrangement of repeating blocks is well suited to this analytical tool. Books and websites that explain symmetry analysis often use quilts as illustrations.[29] Noted quiltmaker Jinny Beyer uses symmetry to teach quilt design, emphasizing parallels to the work of Dutch artist M.C. Escher.[30]

Some scholars have noted that irregularities in what would otherwise be symmetrical patterns in textiles pose a problem in the classification of symmetry. Washburn and Crowe define minor pattern irregularities as either unintentional or intentional.[31] Using an appliquéd rose quilt as an example, they suggest that such irregularities should be ignored because the dominant symmetry is still apparent. Bier, who noted irregularities in both pattern and color in oriental carpets, termed the phenomenon "symmetry-breaking" or "broken symmetry."[32] She attributed symmetry-breaking to the slight variations resulting from the imprecision of cloth production, noting that these minor differences make carpets more interesting visually. On the symmetry website, Bier states:

Symmetry-breaking exists where a symmetry is expected, but the expectation is not met. As we often see with Oriental carpets, it is a playfulness with symmetry that results in intriguing patterns. In nature, symmetry is imperfect, although mathematicians treat it as an ideal. In art, too, it seems that approximation of symmetry, rather than its precision, teases the mind as it pleases the eye.[33]

Because textiles rarely display evenly distributed combinations of two, three, or four colors, many researchers who have applied symmetry analysis to textiles do not use the two-color pattern classification system proposed by Washburn and Crow. Peter Stevens, who authored the *Handbook of Regular Patterns*, did not include color symmetries, although he mentioned color.

Method

In this study, symmetry analysis was applied to the quilts in the Sara Miller Collection using the notation system in Washburn and Crowe's *Symmetries of Culture*. In a quilt, symmetrical arrangements of design elements can be found in several components. Most obvious is the design arrangement on the face of the quilt. Symmetry arrangements in quilts may be classified as finite designs (e.g., medallion quilts), bands of one-dimensional designs (e.g., strip quilts), or two-dimensional planes (e.g., block style quilts). When two or more colors are evenly distributed in the patterns, symmetry of color is possible. Like Oriental carpets, quilts may have designs in both the field and the border. When borders display symmetrical pattern arrangements, a separate notation was assigned to the border pattern.

Quilts also display symmetry in quilting patterns when the stitches form motifs. The possibilities for symmetrical arrangements in quilting patterns include all three of the basic symmetry classes. When quilting follows the outline of a medallion format, the pattern is a finite design. When a quilting pattern is confined to a border or strip, the design is one-dimensional. If the quilting pattern develops around a block format, the pattern is two-dimensional. Symmetry of quilting pattern was noted separately for the field and for the one or more borders on the face of the quilt.

For each quilt, this analysis addressed the following questions:
- Does the face of the quilt exhibit a symmetrical arrangement in the piecing?
- If so, is it a finite design, a one-dimensional design, or a two-dimensional design (or a combination if both field and border are pieced)? Within each of these classes, what is the notation?
- Does the quilting pattern display a finite design, a one-dimensional design, or a two-dimensional design? What is the notation?
- Are colors equally distributed? If so, what is the notation for the color symmetry?
- If symmetry is irregular, what observations can be made regarding the broken symmetry?

Three methodological challenges occurred in applying symmetry analysis to the Sara Miller Collection. The first challenge was to determine the unit of analysis. As Bier noted in her study of Oriental carpets, "visual analysis of pattern is a process requiring patience and curiosity on the part of the viewer . . . Initially the process of 'reading' a pattern is not self-evident."[34] In a quilt, the basic unit could be an individual patch, a block, or a part of a finite design. Quilters build patterns through joining individual pieces of fabric to form strips, blocks, or other geometric shapes, eventually achieving a quilt top. The unit of analysis may or may not align with the piecing sequence. In the Hole in the Barn Door pictured in Plate 55, each block has four sets of mirror axes. As seen in the diagram (Figure 14), the unit of analysis is one-eighth of the pieced block. Thus, the quilt belongs to the *p4m* classification of two-dimensional patterns.

The second challenge involved determining if symmetry was present despite slight variations, which included irregular sizes of patches and irregular use of color. Perception plays a critical role in our reading a quilt's symmetry. Our eyes want to see the repetitions and accommodate for slight irregularities in color and patch size. The Basket quilt in Plate 56, for example, is not truly symmetrical because of the irregular use of color in the baskets, yet we still view the overall arrangement of the baskets as symmetrical because eight of the 12 baskets are identically colored. The inner border of Plate 56, however, is asymmetrical both for size of patch and placement of color. (I counted the field, but not the border, as symmetrical for this quilt.)

The third challenge involved classifying incomplete, or truncated designs, where the quiltmaker intended a certain configuration but was restricted by the size of the finished quilt. The Log Cabin (Barnraising variation) in Plate 57 is an example. As suggested by Washburn and Crowe, I classified truncated designs as if the pattern repeated to infinity.[35]

Symmetry in the Sara Miller Collection of Amish Crib Quilts

The 90 Amish crib quilts in the Sara Miller Collection exhibit symmetry in all three areas—finite designs, one-dimensional patterns, and two-dimensional patterns—on both their face sides and in their quilting. Looking first at the quilt face, 21 quilts (23%) display asymmetrical pattern arrangements and thus have no symmetry in their designs (see Figure 15, page 74). The asymmetry results from either irregularly sized patches, or from the absence of color repetition.

(continued on page 74)

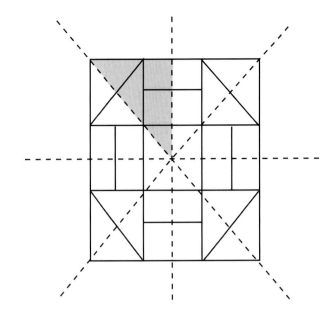

Figure 14

Diagram of a block from Hole in the Barn Door (Plate 55) illustrating how a design is broken down for symmetry analysis.

Plate 55
Hole in the Barn Door
Mrs. Levi Bontrager
1920-1940
Probably made in Indiana
37.5" x 29.5"
Cottons
QSPI: 7-8
International Quilt Study Center,
Sara Miller Collection, 2000.007.0058

Despite this quiltmaker's use of a variety of fabric pieces, the quilt has a deliberate design that features two long sashing strips and two center blocks pieced from the same dark blue fabric. The quiltmaker used an atypical fabric—a purple seersucker, a cloth with a distinct pucker—in some of the blocks. Each Hole in the Barn Door block has four sets of mirror axes, revealing both vertical and horizontal reflection.

Plate 56
Baskets
Maker unknown • 1920-1940 • Possibly made in Arthur, Illinois • 49" x 38.5"
Cottons • QSPI: 7-8
International Quilt Study Center, Sara Miller Collection, 2000.007.0028

The Baskets and strip-pieced border in this quilt are set against a striking black ground, assembled from several different fabrics, including cotton sateen. The practice of using several different fabric types of the same (or similar) color to create a design or ground is commonly found in the Miller Collection, as well as in many full-size Amish quilts of the same period. This quiltmaker saw no need to purchase black yardage of the same fabric for the background, when she had enough of several different pieces of black fabric to make do. The irregular use of color in the Basket blocks prevents this quilt from being truly symmetrical.

Plate 57
Log Cabin, Barn Raising variation
Maker unknown • 1920-1940 • Possibly made in Holmes County, Ohio • 47" x 36"
Cottons • QSPI: 7
International Quilt Study Center, Sara Miller Collection, 2000.007.0079

This Barn Raising variation of the Log Cabin pattern is pieced from what may have been fabric used to make men's work clothes, including some denim. Amish men usually wear "barndoor" pants, featuring a wide front flap that conceals the button fly and front pockets. The symmetry of this pattern is restricted by the rectangular shape of the finished quilt; thus, the design is truncated.

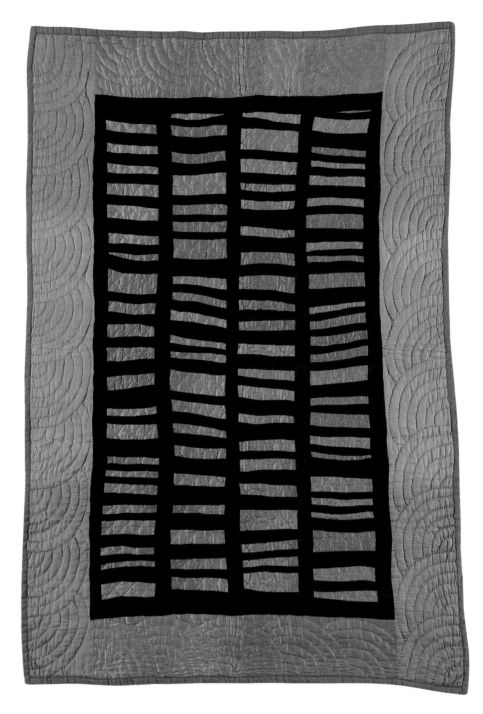

Plate 58
Chinese Coins
Maker unknown • 1920-1940 • Made in Midwestern United States; acquired in Clark, Missouri
46.5" x 32" • Cottons • QSPI: 7
International Quilt Study Center, Sara Miller Collection, 2000.007.0025

    This two-color Chinese Coin quilt glows, due to the use of cotton sateen, a cotton cloth woven with a satin weave that produces a distinct sheen. Sateens were popular among both Amish and mainstream quiltmakers during the second quarter of the twentieth century. While this quilt features bold, dark colors, soft pastel sateens were fashionable in "English" quilts of the 1920s and 1930s. An asymmetrical design results from the use of the uneven strips used to piece the bars.

Plate 59
One Patch
Maker unknown • 1910-1930 • Possibly made in Plain City, Ohio • 39.5" x 35"
Cottons • QSPI: 7-9
International Quilt Study Center, Sara Miller Collection, 2000.007.0050

Four red squares jump out of the sea of blues and tans found in the design field of this quilt. The playful placement of these four squares begs knowledge of this quiltmaker's intentions. The design is considered asymmetrical, due to the random placement of colors.

Symmetry Type	Distribution	Frequency
No symmetry	21	23%
Finite designs	26	29%
One-dimensional patterns (borders)	3	3%
Two-dimensional patterns (all-over designs, planes)	40	45%
Two-color two-dimensional patterns	10	11%

Figure 15

Dominant type of symmetry in quilt face (n=90).

In Plate 58, a Chinese Coins quilt, the uneven strips cancel out the symmetry, despite the overall unity provided by the two alternating colors. In Plate 59, a One Patch, the patches are identical in size, but the random placement of the hues negates any symmetry in the field. The color irregularity resulting from the string method of piecing both the stars and the borders in Plate 60 eliminates the radial symmetry of the two stars. The same is true of the Fans quilt in Plate 61 and the Buzz Saw quilt in Plate 62.

The remaining 69 quilts have one of the three types of symmetrical arrangements on their face sides. Finite designs—quilts in the framed center format—comprise 29 percent of the 90 quilts (26 quilts). Designs composed of patterned strips in which the design repeats at least once are represented by just three quilts (3%).[36] (This number does not include the two quilts with patterned borders.) Block patterns, which are classified as two-dimensional designs because of the all-over pattern arrangement, dominate the other categories with 40 of the 90 quilts (45%). When two colors are evenly dis-

tributed in sections of block format quilts, symmetrical arrangements occur. Color symmetry was observed in 10 of the 90 quilts, comprising 11% of the total.

The symmetry types found for the quilting designs are seen in Figure 16. Since quilting on Amish quilts does not necessarily follow the pattern of the pieced face of the quilt, the distribution of symmetry types for quilting is much different than the symmetries for the face of the quilt. Many quilts have more than one border, each quilted in a different pattern. Thus, the total occurrences of one-dimensional patterns (109) exceed the number of quilts (90). Quilting in strip or border designs (one-dimensional patterns) occurs most frequently. Quilting that follows the block format of the face design appears in 54 quilts. Finite designs in which the quilting rotates around a central point appear in 21 quilts. All but one quilt displays some symmetry in their quilting patterns. The one that does not is quilted in straight lines that form a grid, but it has no repetition of motifs. (A single straight line by itself is not a figure or motif.)

(continued on page 77)

Symmetry Type	Distribution
No symmetry	1
Finite designs	21
One-dimensional patterns (borders)	109
Two-dimensional patterns (all-over designs, planes)	54

Figure 16

Type of symmetry in quilting.

Plate 60
String Stars
Maker unknown
1930-1950
Made in Kalona, Iowa
35" x 27"
Cottons, a bit of wool, a bit of wool/cotton mixture
QSPI: 7-8
International Quilt Study Center,
Sara Miller Collection, 2000.007.0075

The fabric used on the back of this playful String Stars quilt is stamped "L.E.Edmundson, Kalona, IA." This is the name of a locally owned department store. On the quilt top, the purple ground fabric sets off the colorful stars and framing strips. The random nature of the string piecing method negates the radial symmetry that would exist with a consistent use of colors.

Plate 61
Fans
Maker unknown
1910-1930
Probably made in Indiana
44.5" x 35.5"
Wools, cottons, wool/cotton mixtures
QSPI: 7-8
International Quilt Study Center,
Sara Miller Collection, 2000.007.0062

The Fan motif became popular during the late nineteenth century because of America's fascination with exotic Eastern cultures. A few decades later, the Amish in northern Indiana developed a particular fondness for the Fan design and created many variations using the traditional Amish color palette. In this quilt, four Fans are pieced together to form a wheel, and the design field is framed by a pieced border that matches the spokes of the expertly pieced wheels. Radial symmetry is negated by the random color placement in both the Fans and the strip border.

75

Plate 62
Buzz Saw
Maker unknown • 1920-1940 • Possibly made in Indiana • 39" x 33" • Cottons • QSPI: 6-7
International Quilt Study Center, Sara Miller Collection, 2000.007.0090

Small triangles set around each diamond in the square seem to be spinning—hence the pattern name, Buzz Saw. Often the sawtooth treatment is pieced from just two alternating colors; however, this quiltmaker incorporated multiple colors, which eliminate the radial symmetry of each block. One block varies from the others because it has a navy blue square at its center, rather than the black square found elsewhere on the quilt's face.

Notation	Quilt Face	Quilting
cn*	0	9
d1	1	0
d2	5	1
d4	20	11
TOTAL	26	21

* n refers to the number of rotations

Figure 17

Distribution of finite designs.

Symmetry in finite designs. As noted above, finite designs appear in both the faces of the quilts and in their quilting designs. The distributions for both can be seen in Figure 17. Finite designs exhibit rotation of identical parts around a center point. The parts also may reflect. None of the quilts exhibit finite designs with rotation symmetry only. A finite design that displays only bilateral reflection is classed as a *d1* design; the Sara Miller Collection includes only one of this symmetry type. It is a Pine Tree (refer to Plate 29). As Janneken Smucker points out (see page 35), this quilt exemplifies a departure from the typical Amish centered format and should be considered an innovation.

Finite designs more commonly display symmetries with rotation, combined with two-fold or four-fold reflection. Designs with two-fold reflection (*d2*) reflect one motif across a vertical axis and another across a horizontal axis. Five quilts display this type of symmetry, as exemplified by the Bars variation (Plate 64). Designs with four-fold reflection (*d4*) reflect the same motif across both the vertical and horizontal axes. Twenty quilts have four-fold reflection, as exemplified by the Star of Bethlehem in Plate 63. The Sunshine and Shadow in Plate 65 is also a four-fold design, despite the truncated arrangement dictated by its rectangular size.

The quilting in the Sara Miller Collection displays three types of finite designs (Figure 17). Nine quilts

Plate 63
Star of Bethlehem
Maker unknown
1930-1950
Made in Midwestern United States
40" x 30"
Cottons
QSPI: 4-6
International Quilt Study Center,
Sara Miller Collection, 2000.007.0011

This quilt shows a quiltmaker in transition away from traditional Amish quilt design. The slightly garish colors do not correspond to the traditional rich, dark colors used in most Amish quilts, or to the soft pastel colors Amish began to adopt in response to trends in the "English" world. The usual defining borders are absent, leaving the star floating in the center of the quilt, another uncharacteristic feature. The single star is an example of a finite design with four-fold reflection.

Plate 64
Bars variation
Maker unknown
1920-1940 • Made in Midwestern United States • 46" x 32" • Cottons • QSPI: 7-8
International Quilt Study Center, Sara Miller Collection, 2000.007.0038

This Bars variation features deep red strips of fabrics running across the narrow width of the quilt. The Bars are "floating"; they are not contained by the typical frames found on most Bars quilts. An unusual design feature of this quilt is the use of shorter strips of fabric that run vertically at the top and bottom of the horizontal strips. This quilt exhibits two-fold reflection, where one pattern is reflected across the vertical axis and another across the horizontal axis.

Plate 65
Sunshine and Shadow
Maker unknown
1910-1930
Possibly made in Arthur, Illinois
33" x 30.5"
Wools, cottons
QSPI: 8
International Quilt Study Center,
Sara Miller Collection, 2000.007.0063

The central portion of this Sunshine and Shadow quilt features an unusual construction technique. A wine-colored, three-inch square is surrounded by right triangles, transforming it into a 5.5-inch center square set on point. Smaller squares in alternating colors form rings around the center, using the typical Sunshine and Shadow construction of alternating light and dark fabrics. This pattern is considered symmetrical, despite the truncated arrangement caused by the quilt's rectangular format.

show rotational symmetry only in quilting; these are primarily feathered wreaths. Only one quilt has a quilting design with a two-fold reflection, while 11 exhibit four-fold reflection designs.

One-dimensional symmetry. One-dimensional patterns appear in both patterned bands and borders on the face of a quilt and in the quilting. One-dimensional designs are much more frequent in quilting than in pieced strips on the face of a quilt (Figure 18). Only five quilts exhibit one-dimensional patterns on their face sides. Four of these are of the same type (*pmm2*), which are comprised of repeating units with reflection in both horizontal and vertical directions. The Bars quilt with three distinct bands of Nine Patch blocks exemplifies this symmetry (Plate 66). Because the design repeats once along a line, the Nine Patch quilt

Notation	Quilt Face	Quilting	TOTAL
p111	1	33	34
p1m	0	5	5
pm11	0	2	2
p112	0	12	12
pmm2	4	37	41
pma2	0	15	15
p1a1	0	5	5
TOTAL	5*	109	114

* This number includes three quilts with patterned fields and two with patterned borders.

Figure 18

Distribution of one-dimensional patterns (borders, bars).

Plate 66
Bars
Maker unknown • 1910-1930 • Possibly made in Indiana • 46.5" x 37"
Cottons • QSPI: 8
International Quilt Study Center, Sara Miller Collection, 2000.007.0007

This quilt combines the design sensibilities of the Midwestern Amish with that of the Lancaster County Amish. The Bars pattern was one of the most commonly used Lancaster County quilt designs. The block format, preferred by many Midwestern Amish quiltmakers, is placed within the Bars design. Quilts with a similar combination of pieced blocks and bars were also made in Lancaster County; Lancaster County variations, however, would likely have had square dimensions and would not have been made in the crib-size format. This quilt exemplifies one-dimensional symmetry in the three bars of Nine Patch blocks.

in Plate 67 is also classified as a one-dimensional design with each block exhibiting vertical and horizontal reflections.

The quilting in the borders displays all seven types of one-dimensional designs (Figure 19). In general, the borders display remarkable variety in quilting patterns. The most common quilting patterns exhibit both vertical and horizontal reflection (*pmm2*), such as cables where the stitches cross each other. Almost as common are simple translations (*p111*) of an asymmetrical motif, such as a rainbow or leaf. Motifs that repeat using vertical reflection with rotation (*pma2*) are in 15 borders, while those that repeat only through rotation (*p112*) appear in 12 borders. Quilting motifs that reflect in only one direction, either vertical (*pm11*) or horizontal (*p1m1*), occur infrequently. Glide reflection (*p1a1*) also is not a common symmetry type in quilting patterns.

Two-dimensional symmetry. Designs that have at least two rows of repeating patterns are considered two-dimensional designs, or all-over designs. Once again,

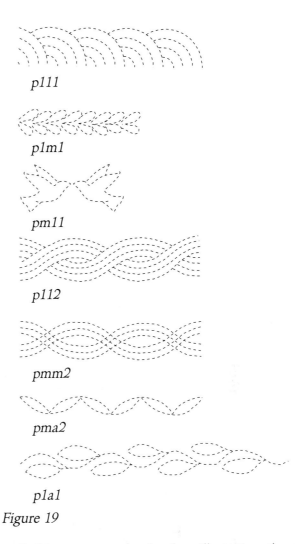

Figure 19

Quilting patterns for borders illustrating the seven one-dimensional arrangements. Patterns taken from quilts in the Sara Miller Collection.

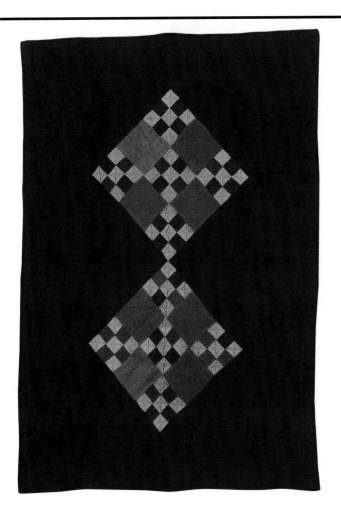

Plate 67
Nine Patch
Maker unknown
1900-1920
Possibly made in Indiana
46.5" x 32"
Wools, cottons
QSPI: 7-9
International Quilt Study Center,
Sara Miller Collection, 2000.007.0052

The maker used three different red fabrics to offset the Nine Patch blocks of this quilt. Red fabric is rarely incorporated into quilts made in several Amish communities, although the Amish in northern Indiana readily accepted the color. Each block exhibits both vertical and horizontal reflection.

81

Plate 68
Stars
Maker unknown • 1910-1930 • Possibly made in Kalona, Iowa • 35.5" x 33.5"
Cottons, wools • QSPI: 5-6
International Quilt Study Center, Sara Miller Collection, 2000.007.0087

This quilt features an extremely low value contrast between the dark blue fabrics and the black ground. The quilting design juxtaposes concentric circles with rigid double-parallel lines. This evenly colored quilt is an example of two-dimensional symmetry with eight-fold reflection.

these symmetries appear in both the quilt face and the quilting patterns (Figure 20). On the face, two-dimensional symmetry occurs in regularly repeating block patterns or wide borders that have at least two rows of a repeating pattern.

The makers of the Sara Miller quilts used only six of the possible 17 two-dimensional symmetries for the fronts of their quilts. By far, the most common two-dimensional patterns have straight rows of motifs with vertical and horizontal reflections, either eight-fold reflection (*p4m*) as seen in the Stars quilt in Plate 68, or four-fold reflection (*pmm*) as seen in the Love Chain in Plate 69 and the Diamonds in Plate 70. Five display motifs with vertical symmetry arranged in straight rows (*pm*), are seen in the Baskets quilt in Plate 71. In two instances, vertically symmetrical motifs appear in an alternating format (*cm*). The Ocean Waves quilt in Plate 72 contains pieced sections in the *cm* classification in both field and border.

Two other arrangements of reflecting or rotating patterns are present, but infrequently (*p2* and *p6m*). Plates 73 and 75 illustrate these less common symmetries.

The Rail Fence in Plate 73 is interesting for the two symmetries exhibited in the face of the quilt: the color-matched rectangles in the field (*p2*) and the checkerboard design of the border (*p4m*). The Stars quilt in Plate 75 is the single example of the *p6m* pattern arrangement.

The all-over quilting patterns display nine types of symmetry (Figure 20). The most common symmetry is an overall diamond pattern (*cmm*), appearing in 21 quilts. Once again, as with the face sides of the quilts, patterns with both vertical and horizontal symmetry (*pmm*) are frequent, with 16 occurrences. The other seven symmetry patterns observed in the quilts appear in five or fewer examples.

Color symmetry. Ten of the 90 quilts display patterns in two colors, either in the blocks, the borders, or over the entire field.[37] To be symmetrical for color, two or more colors must be distributed in equal proportions among the repeating motifs. Of the 46 possible color arrangements they could have chosen, makers of the Sara Miller quilts employed six of the arrangements.[38] Plate 74, a Tulip quilt that illustrates

Plate 69
Love Chain
Maker unknown
1910-1930
Possibly made in Michigan
45.5" x 35.5"
Cottons, wool/cotton mixture (pink)
QSPI: 7-8
International Quilt Study Center,
Sara Miller Collection, 2000.007.0081

The combination of bold pink, red, and black might have seemed incongruous to a mainstream quiltmaker's sense of color, but such combinations are not uncommon on Amish quilts. Amish quiltmakers often pair hues in ways not found in quilts made by the "English." The relative isolation of the Amish from the trends and fads of fashion helped spur such creative color juxtapositions. The design is an example of two-dimensional symmetry with a four-fold reflection.

Plate 70
Diamonds
Mrs. Amos Bontrager (second wife)
1930-1950
Probably made in Haven, Kansas
43" x 40" • Cottons
QSPI: 7-8
International Quilt Study Center,
Sara Miller Collection, 2000.007.0047

These two quilts are connected by a story that traveled with the quilts to Sara Miller. The red Baskets quilt was made by a Mrs. Amos Bontrager for her daughter. Unfortunately, this Mrs. Bontrager died while still a young mother. Later, her daughter made a Flower Garden quilt. Her stepmother, the second Mrs. Amos Bontrager, using the scraps from the Flower Garden quilt, pieced the Diamonds quilt for her step-grandchild.

Due to the nature of the Amish community, it is difficult to confirm this story by simply tracing genealogical records. Bontrager, like Yoder, Miller, and Stoltzfus, is a very common name among the Old Order Amish, particularly in the Kansas settlement where this quilt was acquired and likely made. Adding to the complexity is the fact that Midwestern Amish families often migrated several times during the course of their lives. For example, Clarence Bontrager, the father of one Amos Bontrager, was born in 1887 in Elkhart County, Indiana. He married in 1908 in Reno County, Kansas, moved to Dodge City, Kansas, in 1909, later moved to a new Amish settlement in Custer County, Oklahoma, and eventually returned to Elkhart County, Indiana, where he is buried.

The Amish continued to migrate throughout the nineteenth and twentieth centuries for a variety of reasons. The desire for affordable farmland has spurred the foundation of some new settlements. Other Amish have migrated to states more open to the Amish education practice of ending formal schooling after the eighth grade. New settlements have been founded to establish a more conservative church discipline, as well as a more modern approach. Amish history is filled with major and minor schisms, and migration has often been a reaction to such religious disagreement.

Plate 71
Baskets
Mrs. Amos Bontrager (first wife)
1900-1920
Probably made in Haven, Kansas
32" x 34" • Cottons
QSPI: 4-5
International Quilt Study Center,
Sara Miller Collection, 2000.007.0030

equal apportionment of red and blue, can be classified as a $c'm$ pattern. Five of the quilts have the same color symmetry pattern $(p_c'4mm)$, which features squares in two colors that alternate in both directions, like a checkerboard. See the Checkerboard design illustrated in Plate 76 for an example of a quilt whose patterning belongs to the $p_c'4mm$ classification. The checkerboard One Patch in Plate 77 displays a variation on two-color symmetry. It has blocks of two-color squares in which one set of squares is consistently colored in all blocks while the other set changes.

Notation	Quilt Face	Quilting	TOTAL
p1	0	0	0
pg	0	0	0
pm	5	2	7
cm	3	1	3
p2	4	5	9
pmm	5	16	21
cmm	0	21	21
pmg	0	0	0
pgg	0	0	0
p4	0	2	2
p4m	24	5	29
p4g	0	0	0
p3	0	0	0
p3m1	0	0	0
p31m	0	1	1
p6	0	0	0
p6m	1	1	2
TOTAL	42*	54	95

* Two quilts have two-dimensional patterns in both the field and the border.

Figure 20

Distribution of two-dimensional patterns (planes, all-over designs).

Discussion and Interpretation

What can we learn about Midwestern Amish quilt-makers' preferences for symmetry by studying the Sara Miller quilts? Furthermore, what do these preferences reflect about Amish culture? Connecting quilts to cultural patterns via symmetry analysis requires a substantial number of quilts from a culture or region. The 90 quilts in the Sara Miller Collection adequately represent Midwestern Amish quilt traditions, even though a few of the patterns seen in other publications about Amish quilts are not represented.

In observing the symmetry preferences for the face sides of the quilts, we see that both finite designs and two-dimensional designs occur often. Finite designs are more frequent in this collection of Midwestern quilts than we would expect, given Granick's comments about how few center format quilts were made outside Pennsylvania. Granick states: "The Medallion pattern, typical to Lancaster County, was uncommon among midwestern Amish quiltmakers."[39] Well over one-fourth of the Sara Miller quilts show symmetries based on a single central point around which motifs rotate and reflect. The explanation might be that these quilts were made by quiltmakers with ties to the Pennsylvania communities; however, this contention is hard to support without knowing the makers and their genealogies. Although the Sara Miller quilts lack careful provenance, most have been attributed to particular Amish settlements, or, at a minimum, to a particular state. As one might imagine, the single quilt from Somerset County in southwestern Pennsylvania, Concentric Squares, is a finite design with a centered format (Plate 78). However, the other finite designs—Sunshine and Shadow, Star of Bethlehem, and the Plain Quilts—come from Ohio, Illinois, Iowa, Indiana, and Wisconsin. None of these finite designs are the Center Diamond quilts we associate with Lancaster County.[40] Their symmetries, however, reveal that they are derivative of the Pennsylvania symmetries, while at the same time expressing a departure from the "mother" designs (See Plate 79).

When employing the repeating block format, makers of quilts in the Sara Miller Collection used a limited number of symmetries. This narrow range of symmetries demonstrates the motions of reflection and rotation, but not of translation or glide reflection. Reflection symmetries are vertical and horizontal, or vertical

(continued on page 93)

85

Plate 72
Ocean Waves
Maker unknown • 1910-1930 • Probably made in Ohio, acquired in Arthur, Illinois
47" x 36.5" • Cottons • QSPI: 8
International Quilt Study Center, Sara Miller Collection, 2000.007.0024

Although this quilt was found in the Arthur, Illinois, Amish settlement, it was probably made in an Ohio Amish community. Due to the migratory nature of the Midwestern Amish, this possibility is not surprising. Several characteristics support the Ohio attribution: the black background, the two-color combination, and the Ocean Waves pattern, a particular favorite of the Ohio Amish. Both the field and border feature vertically symmetrical motifs.

Plate 73
Rail Fence
Maker unknown • 1920-1940 • Possibly made in Ohio • 44.5" x 34" • Cottons • QSPI: 7
International Quilt Study Center, Sara Miller Collection, 2000.007.0034

The inner border of this quilt is formed by a checkerboard of alternating black and blue squares. The quilt gradually increases in intensity, beginning with the solid black border and ending with the busy, multicolored zigzags of the Rail Fence design. Two symmetries appear in the design of the quilt top, one in the checkerboard border and one in the color-matched rectangles in the field.

Plate 74
Tulip
Maker unknown • 1910-1930 • Possibly made in Arthur, Illinois • 38" x 33" • Cottons • QSPI: 7
International Quilt Study Center, Sara Miller Collection, 2000.007.0082

This unusual repeated block resembles a stylized tulip, or a downward pointing arrow, that creates diagonal motion across the plane of the quilt. The quiltmaker further enlivened her design by using red thread to quilt simple chevrons in the design field and cables in the borders. The equal apportionment of red and blue exemplifies a form of color symmetry.

Plate 75
Stars
Maker unknown
1940-1960
Possibly made in Independence, Iowa
40" x 28.5"
Cottons
QSPI: 7
International Quilt Study Center,
Sara Miller Collection, 2000.007.0043

This quilt is pieced from a combination of 60-degree diamonds and octagons, similar to those used to piece the popular "English" Grandmother's Flower Garden quilts of the 1930s. The binding of a second quilt can be felt through the exterior of this quilt, indicating that the quiltmaker may have recycled an old quilt as batting.

Plate 76
Checkerboard
Maker unknown
1920-1940
Possibly made in Holmes County, Ohio
30" x 26.5"
Cottons
QSPI: 6-7
International Quilt Study Center,
Sara Miller Collection, 2000.007.0065

This unusual design features a checkerboard of blue and black squares, set on point in a format similar to the Lancaster County Center Diamond design (see Figure 4). Sixteen Patch blocks pieced from identical blue and black squares frame the central design. This alternation of colors creates a symmetrically colored pattern. Despite the general preference of Midwestern Amish quiltmakers for block format quilts, they sometimes incorporated the medallion-style format in innovative ways in their creation of crib quilts.

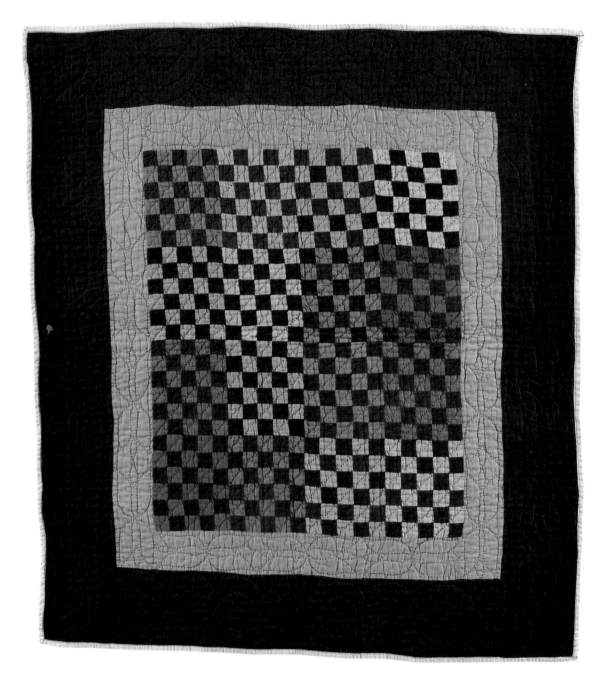

Plate 77

One Patch

Maker unknown • 1930-1950 • Possibly made in Indiana • 34" x 30.5"
Cottons, a bit of wool • QSPI: 7-11
International Quilt Study Center, Sara Miller Collection, 2000.007.0076

This quilt could be called a "Thirty Patch"; 30 small patches of alternating bright hues and black ground form the blocks that result in a variation of two-color symmetry. Quilted into the blue inner frame of this quilt is a simplified tulip design. The tulip is one of the most common symbols seen in Pennsylvania German folk art and is often featured prominently in Pennsylvania German appliqué quilts, as well as being subtly stitched into Amish quilting designs.

Plate 78
Concentric Squares
Maker unknown • 1910-1930 • Possibly made in Somerset County, Pennsylvania
43.5" x 43.5" • Cottons • QSPI: 8
International Quilt Study Center, Sara Miller Collection, 2000.007.0060

While multiple frames and borders are not an uncommon feature of Amish quilts, this quilt-maker took the practice a step further. Each colored frame alternates with a black frame as each decreases in width toward the center. The quilting design, however, disregards the frames. Juxtaposed with the rigid concentric lines of the frames are circular rings of feathers and cross-hatching. The pieced top is an example of a finite design with a centered format.

Plate 79
Baskets
Maker unknown • 1910-1930 • Possibly made in Arthur, Illinois • 34" x 33"
Cottons, wools, wool/cotton mixtures • QSPI: 8
International Quilt Study Center, Sara Miller Collection, 2000.007.0040

Four Basket blocks are each oriented toward the center of the quilt to form this unusual design. The maker pieced the quilt from a variety of quality fabrics, including black cotton sateen, red twill dress wool, and a tan wool and cotton mixture. This use of fine fabrics is characteristic of quiltmakers from the Amish settlement near Arthur, Illinois. The symmetry of this quilt suggests a link to the centered format associated with quilts of the Lancaster County Amish.

only. The arrangements in the overall patterns more often have a straight set, rather than being set on point, as is done in many other American quilts. These preferences reveal that Amish quiltmakers selected easy-to-comprehend symmetries for the visible side of their quilts. Washburn points out that humans most easily perceive symmetry across a vertical axis because we ourselves are vertical in orientation.[41] The next most salient symmetry is that which occurs across a horizontal axis; this symmetry is almost nonexistent in the Sara Miller quilts. More difficult to perceive are symmetries across diagonal lines, which also appear infrequently in these quilts. When mirror symmetry is absent, the eye focuses on the center of rotationally symmetric motifs, as in the quilts with finite, or center format, designs.

Some might argue that most American quilts in the block style have reflection and rotation symmetry. However, a number of symmetries common to non-Amish quilts are not seen in the Sara Miller quilts. For example, simple translation of an asymmetrical motif across a plane (p1) and repetition of rotating motifs across a plane (p3, p4, p6) are missing from this group of quilts. The Eagle quilt in Figure 21 exhibits translation symmetry for both the field and the border: the asymmetrical eagles repeat in two directions in the field, and in one direction around the border. The Princess Feather quilt in Figure 22 illustrates rotational symmetry in the four large designs: each of the feathers rotates around the center star four times, a p4 arrangement. The Pellmans illustrate a few p4 arrangements in their books on Amish quilts—Pinwheel and Drunkard's Path—indicating that at least a few Amish women used rotational symmetry when piecing their quilts.[42]

Figure 21
Eagles
Maker unknown
Possibly made in Cherrytree County, Pennsylvania
1870-1890 • 78" x 73" • Cottons • QSPI: 9-10
International Quilt Study Center,
Ardis and Robert James Collection, 1997.007.0126

This quilt exhibits translation symmetry in both the field and the border. Translation symmetry across a plane is not present in the Sara Miller Collection.

Figure 22
Princess Feather
M. Gingrich
Probably made in Dauphin County, Pennsylvania
Dated 1954 • 85" x 84" • Cottons • QSPI: 5-6
International Quilt Study Center,
Ardis and Robert James Collection, 1997.007.0774

This quilt exhibits rotational symmetry. None of the quilts in the Sara Miller Collection display rotational symmetry on the face of the quilt.

Plate 80
Bars
Maker unknown
1920-1940
Probably made in Arthur, Illinois
46" x 39"
Cottons
QSPI: 6-8
International Quilt Study Center,
Sara Miller Collection, 2000.007.0083

Although this quilt was likely made in the Amish settlement of Arthur, Illinois, it resembles Bars quilts commonly made in the Lancaster County, Pennsylvania Amish settlement. The Lancaster variation typically has square dimensions, is framed with proportionally wider borders, and is pieced with dress wools. This version is pieced from cotton and features a narrow border and a rectangular format. Notice the use of four different quilting patterns in three different symmetries, quilted into the strips and borders.

The real surprise comes in the quilting patterns. More symmetry types occur in the one-dimensional patterns selected for the borders than for the face designs. All seven classes of one-dimensional patterns are found in the borders. Quilters used more than one symmetry type in a single quilt by stitching each of the borders in a different pattern. Some have three or more symmetry classifications represented in a single quilt. For example, the Bars quilt in Plate 80 is simply constructed, but the multiple strips offered the quiltmaker the opportunity to use four different quilting patterns in three different symmetries to stitch her quilt together (*pmm2, pma2,* and *p112*).

The quiltmakers could have quilted quickly in allover patterns instead of using the elaborate stitching seen in the Sara Miller quilts, especially considering that the quilts were intended for hard use as young children's bed covers. Only one of the quilts appears to have been quilted in a hurry (see Janneken Smucker essay and Plate 49). It is a simple One Patch, for which the quilter used blue pearl cotton instead of quilting thread. No overall pattern to the quilting is evident; just rows of straight lines.

The wide range of one-dimensional symmetries in the quilted borders suggests that Amish women found

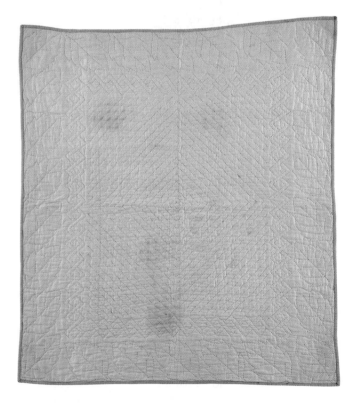

Figure 23

Reverse side of quilt pictured in Plate 81.

Plate 81
Sunshine and Shadow
Maker unknown • 1920-1940 • Possibly made in Ohio • 37" x 33.5" • Cottons
QSPI: 6-7
International Quilt Study Center, Sara Miller Collection, 2000.007.0001

This bold Sunshine and Shadow quilt exhibits the Midwestern Amish practice of juxtaposing bright jewel-toned hues against a black or dark blue background. The black border, however, hides the decorative quilting stitches that depict a row of floating leaves. The quilt's back is a bright lemon yellow, which, because of the contrast, shows off the quilting stitches. The quilt is an example of four-fold reflection.

Plate 82
Broken Dishes
Maker unknown • 1920-1940 • Possibly made in Indiana • 38" x 34" • Cottons • QSPI: 6-8
International Quilt Study Center, Sara Miller Collection, 2000.007.0037

Broken Dishes and other patterns incorporating small pieced triangles, such as Birds in Air and Ocean Waves, were very popular among Midwestern Amish quiltmakers. Unlike their Lancaster County cousins who pieced quilts featuring large blocks intended to showcase quilting stitches, the Midwestern Amish favored intricately pieced designs. This maker, however, combined intricate piecing with decorative quilting designs—clamshells, circles, and double lines—that display an assortment of symmetries when viewed on the light-colored backing fabric.

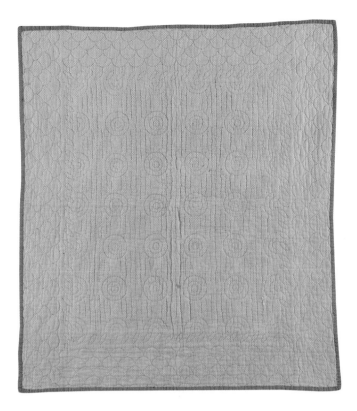

Figure 24

Reverse side of quilt pictured in Plate 82.

an outlet for creativity in quilting rather than piecing. The *Ordnung* specified the use of solid colors, and in some conservative communities prohibited piecing and multi-colored patterns.[43] Certainly appliquéd designs were out of the question because they wasted fabric. Quilting patterns apparently did not come under scrutiny, although "showy" quilting might have been considered prideful. Because the dark quilting thread renders the quilting stitches nearly invisible on the front of the quilt, the quilting shows primarily on the back where few people see it.

The reverse sides of these quilts are spectacular, particularly when the backing fabric is light in color. The back of a Sunshine and Shadow quilt from Ohio, illustrates this (Plate 81 and Figure 23, front and back). Nearly square in shape, it has a centered design. The dark stitching, easily visible on the yellow backing fabric, reveals three types of symmetry: a finite design, and two one-dimensional designs, including an outer border of carefully stitched leaves. The leaves display translation symmetry, a motion that is not present in the face designs. Another intricately quilted piece is

seen in Figure 24. This quilting pattern, based on the block format, shows a clamshell pattern, along with circles and double lines. The quilting design bears little relationship to the design on the face of the quilt (Plate 82). The full array of symmetries in the quilting suggests that Amish women expressed their creativity in stitching together tops, battings, and backs.

The limited number of quilts with color symmetry is not surprising, because most Amish quiltmakers used scraps when cutting fabrics for their quilts. This accounts for the many quilts with color irregularities. When hue and value are very close, the colors appear to be symmetrically arranged, even though they are not exactly symmetrical. For example, the Bow Tie quilt in Plate 83 is comprised of several shades of two main colors—pink and maroon—but because the human eye accommodates for near symmetries, this quilt may be classed as a two-color quilt with the notation $p_c'4mm$. Another explanation for the limited use of color symmetry is that many quilt patterns do not have equal spaces for alternating colors.

Symmetry-breaking deserves comment. Only about a third of the quilts (32 out of 90) are absolutely symmetrical. This number includes truncated designs that technically exhibit incomplete symmetry, such as Sunshine and Shadow and Log Cabin, but are otherwise symmetrical. Symmetry-breaking is one of the features that makes Amish quilts so visually interesting. Expected symmetries would be boring. For example, the Stars quilt in Plate 84 repeats the shape of the design, but not the colors. If we disregard the color, the pattern arrangement exhibits four-fold reflection (*p4m*). The irregularity of the rich colors in the stars draws the viewer's attention and holds it, whereas same-color stars would render the symmetries in the design so easily perceived that the eye would move on to something else. Another example of symmetry-breaking is seen in Plate 85. The small pink blocks interrupt the uniformity of the dominant black blocks in both size and color. In many of the Sara Miller quilts, as in the Star quilt in Plate 86, color is the reason a quilt is not perfectly symmetrical, despite repeating patterns.

The many quilts with reflection and rotation symmetries exhibited in both the finite designs and the two-dimensional block patterns focus inward toward a single center, or toward multiple, repeated centers. Visible on the fronts of the quilts, these tightly ordered

(continued on page 103)

Plate 83
Bow Tie
Maker unknown • 1920-1940 • Possibly made in Holmes County, Ohio • 53" x 38"
Cottons • QSPI: 5-7
International Quilt Study Center, Sara Miller Collection, 2000.007.0041

This quilt is composed of fabrics of various weaves in several shades of the two main colors, pink and maroon. Despite the use of different shades, the two-color design appears symmetrical because the maker chose fabrics close in hue and value.

Plate 84
Stars
Maker unknown
1920-1940
Possibly made in Wisconsin
36" x 32"
Cottons
QSPI: 8-9
International Quilt Study Center,
Sara Miller Collection, 2000.007.0067

Due to the absence of an interior frame, the stars in this quilt float on a field of black. The maker placed the bright contrasting stars randomly, with the lone gold star attracting particular attention. The varied colors of the stars break the symmetry of the design, but when color is disregarded, the pattern exhibits four-fold reflection. The eight-pointed Star motif is repeated in the quilting of the black setting squares.

Plate 85
Square in a Square
Maker unknown
1920-1940
Possibly made in Indiana
37" x 29"
Cottons
QSPI: 7-8
International Quilt Study Center,
Sara Miller Collection, 2000.007.0086

The creative design of this quilt features small pink and black blocks in the sashing intersections, which echo the larger black and blue blocks. The inclusion of these pink blocks results in broken symmetry. The block design itself is also unusual, perhaps an invention of the quiltmaker.

Plate 86
Stars
Maker unknown • 1910-1930 • Possibly made in Ohio • 33.5" x 33" • Cottons • QPSI: 7-8
International Quilt Study Center, Sara Miller Collection, 2000.007.0056

The black sashing and border of this Stars quilt contrast sharply with the very faded blue and gray fabrics used to piece the blocks. The inconsistent use of color prevents the quilt from being perfectly symmetrical. The back of this quilt is pieced with a simple central square of gray twill cotton fabric, framed by a black border. Reversible quilts, particularly with a simple framed design, are not uncommon in the Ohio Amish settlements.

Plate 87
Star of Bethlehem
Maker unknown
1930-1950
Probably made in Wisconsin
48.5" x 47.5"
Cottons
QSPI: 8
International Quilt Study Center,
Sara Miller Collection, 2000.007.0072

These Star of Bethlehem quilts were made by sisters (according to dealer information), likely in an Amish settlement in Wisconsin. The two quilts are nearly identical, although one has a blue ground and the other a black. The quilts share the same rose, pink, and lavender cotton fabrics; the construction of an inner frame from leftover diamonds used to piece the stars; and identical symmetries in both the pieced tops and the quilted designs. The sisters used identical quilting patterns, varying only in their choices of quilting thread. One used white thread throughout; the other used white on the pastel colors and black on the ground.

Plate 88
Star of Bethlehem
Maker unknown
1930-1950
Probably made in Wisconsin
49" x 47"
Cottons
QSPI: 7
International Quilt Study Center,
Sara Miller Collection, 2000.007.0073

Plate 89
Bricks
Maker unknown
1920-1940
Probably made in Independence
or Oelwein, Iowa
46.5" x 33.5"
Cottons
QSPI: 6
International Quilt Study Center,
Sara Miller Collection, 2000.007.0020

According to dealer information, these two quilts were made by sisters. Rather than randomly piecing together the bits of fabric (as in the quilts featured in Plates 13, 30, and 59), the bricks were assembled together in diagonal rows of color. The quilts are nearly identical in construction and design, differing only in color and quilting designs used in the borders.

Plate 90
Bricks
Maker unknown
1920-1940
Probably made in Independence or Oelwein, Iowa
45" x 33"
Cottons
QSPI: 7
International Quilt Study Center,
Sara Miller Collection, 2000.007.0021

symmetry arrangements are like the Amish communities themselves. The concept of *Gelassenheit*, which Donald Kraybill terms the "cornerstone of Amish values," offers an explanation in culture for the symmetry preferences in the Sara Miller crib quilts.[44] *Gelassenheit* stands for obedience, humility, and simplicity. It means yielding to a higher authority. It entails self-surrender, self-denial, and contentment. Personalities that are quiet and reserved, placing the needs of others above the self, are extolled. Humility, the opposite of pride, is admired. Simplicity is seen as the antithesis of showy, gaudy design. Obedience is the pathway to conformity. The predominance of the center-focused symmetries symbolizes these values, as do the many block-style quilts with vertical and horizontal reflection symmetries. On the surface, each part reflects the whole. Yet the individual urge for creative expression reveals itself in the varieties of symmetries seen in the subtle quilting, the intricacy of which is only apparent from viewing the backs of the quilts.

Another way that *Gelassenheit* is represented in quilts is through repetition of patterns from quilt to quilt; thus, repetition of symmetries. This interpretation is borne out by two pairs of quilts made by sisters. Two sisters in Wisconsin made one of the pairs. The sisters' quilts, both in the Star of Bethlehem pattern, are identical in all respects except for the use of slightly different colors (see Plates 87 and 88). The symmetries are the same for the pieced tops (*d4*) and the quilting (*p112*). A second pair of quilts made by sisters came from the Independence/Oelwin settlements of Iowa (see Plates 89 and 90). Both are in the Bricks pattern, a *p2* classification. Although color use and quilting pattern differ between the two quilts, when viewed together, each quilt repeats the other's pattern and symmetry, as does the pair of Star of Bethlehem quilts. These pairs of nearly identical quilts reveal that both sets of sisters opted for conformity instead of individuality in making their quilts, as would be expected of Amish women.

In conclusion, symmetry analysis of the quilts in the Sara Miller Collection proves an effective tool to explore the intersection of art and culture. Through a formal analysis of a single design principle, we have seen that these Amish quiltmakers preferred a narrow range of symmetries when piecing the fronts of their quilts, which expressed their core values. The full range and variety of symmetries seen in the quilting designs reveals that quilting—the act of stitching together the top, bat, and back—offered Amish women an expanded outlet for creative expression. Because the subtle quilting stitches were not as visible on the front of a quilt, the community accepted the practice of elaborate quilting.

The preponderance of finite designs, said to be uncommon among Midwestern Amish quilters, implies that some currently held perceptions about the differences between Midwestern and Pennsylvania Amish quilts should be revised.

Lastly, the symmetry-breaking caused by slight irregularities in patch size, color, and placement contributes to the exceptional visual appeal of Amish quilts.

AFTERWORD

by Janneken Smucker

The essay, "At the Crossing: Midwestern Amish Crib Quilts and the Intersection of Cultures," (pages 21-62) and the exhibition with the same name, are the culmination of my master's degree in Textile History and Quilt Studies at the University of Nebraska-Lincoln. My curatorial work has combined my interest in quilts and quiltmaking with my interest in a cultural group linked with my own. I grew up in a Mennonite family; Mennonites are religious cousins of the Amish. When my ancestors first immigrated to North America in the eighteenth century, they were part of the larger migration of Amish families to the New World in search of economic and religious freedoms.

Most members of today's Mennonite church no longer exhibit the outward distinctiveness of the Old Order Amish. While my dress and mode of transportation do not separate me from the rest of society, I have been taught to understand the phrase, "in the world, but not of it." Both the Amish and their more change-minded cousins, the Mennonites, use those words to describe their position within society.

With my religious background, I occupy a space on the periphery of the inside. I have a certain amount of "insider knowledge" which allows me to use *The Sugarcreek Budget,* Charm, Ohio, and barndoor pants as points of reference. But while working on this project, I have often found myself counting back the generations to determine which of my ancestors in the mid-nineteenth century decided to become Amish-Mennonites rather than staying with the Old Order Amish. And I often ask, what if their decision had been otherwise? Would I care about quilts? Or would I be like the many Amish women who, as Sara Miller said, "get married young and . . . couldn't care less about the older things."

The choice to liberalize, made five generations back by Isaac Schmucker, an Amish bishop who led the progressive movement in northern Indiana, helped enable me now to pursue graduate studies in textile history and quilt studies. This project has given me a new appreciation of my cultural heritage. I am indebted to my foreparents, such as Bishop Schmucker, and to the generations of prolific quiltmakers, including Magdalena Stutzman, Mary Beechy, and Esther McDowell, who came before me.

Thank you first of all to the International Quilt Study Center (IQSC) and its staff for allowing me the pleasurable experience of serving as graduate curatorial assistant during the past two years. The support, feedback, and wealth of knowledge possessed by Professor Patricia Crews, IQSC director, Carolyn Ducey, IQSC curator, and assistant curator Marin Hanson, has been invaluable.

Sara Miller's willingness to let me visit and interview her in her home in Kalona gave this book a depth that it would otherwise lack. Thank you to the Lincoln Quilters' Guild for their scholarship support which enabled me to visit Ms. Miller. I have relished the opportunity to collaborate with Dr. Linda Welters on this project; her advice and experience have helped greatly. The staff at the Mennonite Historical Library in Goshen, Indiana, has given me much needed advice and expertise in researching the Old Order Amish. I also appreciate the members of my graduate committee, Professors Patricia Crews, Nancy Miller, and Lynne Ireland, for their ongoing feedback.

I have valued the willingness of my Textile History classmates to brainstorm, proofread, and tolerate me as I've worked on this project. And finally, none of this would be possible without the endless support of my parents, George and Barbara Smucker, and my husband, Rick Sieber.

ENDNOTES

"At the Crossing" (pages 21-62)

[1] Sara Miller purchased most of the quilts in this collection from one dealer. This dealer often revealed in what settlement he acquired a quilt, but seldom gave any additional attribution information, including the quilt's maker.

[2] Steven M. Nolt, *A History of the Amish* (Intercourse, Pa.: Good Books, 1992), 9-10.

[3] David Luthy, "Amish Migration Patterns: 1972-1992," in *The Amish Struggle with Modernity*, ed. Donald B. Kraybill and Marc A. Olshan (Hanover: University Press of New England, 1994), 243-259.

[4] Nolt, *A History of the Amish*, 140.

[5] John A. Hostetler, *Amish Society*, 4th ed. (Baltimore: Johns Hopkins University Press, 1993), 97.

[6] Nolt, *A History of the Amish*, 284.

[7] Luthy, "Amish Migration Patterns," 244-245.

[8] Marc A. Olshan, "Conclusion: What Good Are the Amish?" in *The Amish Struggle with Modernity*, ed. Donald B. Kraybill and Marc A. Olshan (Hanover: University Press of New England, 1994), 232.

[9] Donald B. Kraybill, *The Riddle of Amish Culture* (Baltimore: Johns Hopkins University Press, 1989), 144, 146.

[10] Donald B. Kraybill, "Plotting Social Change Across Four Affiliations," in *The Amish Struggle with Modernity*, ed. Donald B. Kraybill and Marc A. Olshan (Hanover: University Press of New England, 1994), 64.

[11] Ibid., 65.

[12] Holstein, "In Plain Sight: The Aesthetics of Amish Quilts," in *A Quiet Spirit: Amish Quilts from the Collection of Cindy Tietze and Stuart Hodosh* (Los Angeles: UCLA Fowler Museum of Cultural History, 1996), 105; Luthy, "Amish Migration Patterns," 243-259.

[13] Eve Wheatcroft Granick, *The Amish Quilt* (Intercourse, Pa.: Good Books, 1989), 30.

[14] Ibid.

[15] Ibid., 106.

[16] Nolt, *A History of the Amish*, 126.

[17] Theron F. Schlabach, *Peace, Faith, Nation: Mennonites and Amish in Nineteenth-Century America* (Scottdale, Pa.: Herald Press, 1988), 218.

[18] Granick also notes the coincidence of the beginnings of Amish quiltmaking and the emergence of the Old Order Amish in *The Amish Quilt*, 39.

[19] Ibid.

[20] Bettina Havig, *Amish Kinder Komforts* (Paducah, Ky.: American Quilter's Society, 1996), 5.

[21] Sara Laurel Holstein, "Sewing and Sowing: Cultural Continuity in an Amish Quilt," in *American Artifacts: Essays in Material Culture*, ed. Jules David Prown and Kenneth Haltman (East Lansing: Michigan State University Press, 2000), 105.

[22] Olshan, "What Good Are the Amish?" 235.

[23] Jonathan Holstein, *The Pieced Quilt: An American Design Tradition* (New York: Viking Books, 1973), 113.

[24] James Christen Steward, foreword to *Amish Quilts 1880 to 1940 from the Collection of Faith and Stephen Brown* (Ann Arbor: University of Michigan Museum of Art, 2000), 6.

[25] Robert Hughes, *Amish: The Art of the Quilt* (New York: Alfred A. Knopf, 1990), 23-24.

[26] David Luthy, "The Origin and Growth of Amish Tourism," in *The Amish Struggle with Modernity*, ed. Donald B. Kraybill and Marc A. Olshan (Hanover: University Press of New England, 1994), 115.

[27] Ibid., 119.

[28] Ibid., 122-129.

[29] David Weaver-Zercher, *The Amish in the American Imagination* (Baltimore: Johns Hopkins University Press, 2001), 83.

[30] Ibid., 85.

[31] Linda Boynton, "Recent Changes in Amish Quiltmaking," in *Uncoverings 1985*, ed. Sally Garoutte (San Francisco, CA: American Quilt Study Group, 1986), 41-42.

[32] Thomas Meyers, "Lunch Pails and Factories," in *The Amish Struggle with Modernity*, ed. Donald B. Kraybill and Marc A. Olshan (Hanover: University Press of New England, 1994), 168; Donald B. Kraybill and Steven M. Nolt, "The Rise of Microenterprises," in *The Amish Struggle with Modernity*, ed. Donald B. Kraybill and Marc A. Olshan (Hanover: University Press of New England, 1994), 150.

[33] Kraybill and Nolt, "The Rise of Microenterprises," 154.

[34] Patricia Herr, "Quilts Within Amish Culture," in *A Quiet Spirit: Amish Quilts from the Collection of Cindy Tietze and Stuart Hodosh* (Los Angeles: UCLA Museum of Cultural History, 1996), 60-62.

[35] Amish and Mennonite Museum Collection records, Goshen College, Goshen, Indiana.

[36] Sara Miller, interview by author, tape recording, Kalona, Iowa, 10 May 2002, International Quilt Study Center, University of Nebraska, Lincoln.

[37] Ibid.

[38] Ibid.

[39] Ibid.

[40] Ibid.

[41] Ibid.

[42] Ibid.

"Symmetry in Amish Quilts" (pages 63-103)

[1] Jonathan Holstein, *American Pieced Quilts* (New York: Viking Press, 1973); Phyllis Haders, *Sunshine and Shadow: The Amish and Their Quilts* (Clinton, N.J.: Main Street Press, 1976); Robert Hughes, *Amish: The Art of the Quilt* (New York: Alfred A. Knopf, 1990); Julie Silber and Eve Wheatcroft Granick, *Amish Quilts of Lancaster County* (San Francisco: M.H. de Young Museum, 1990).

[2] David Weaver-Zercher, *The Amish in the American Imagination* (Baltimore: Johns Hopkins University Press, 2001).

[3] David Luthy, "Amish Migration Patterns: 1972-1992," in *The Amish Struggle with Modernity*, ed. Donald B. Kraybill and Marc

A. Olshan (Hanover: University Press of New England, 1994), 243-259.

⁴ Donald B. Kraybill, "The Quiltwork of Amish Culture," in *A Quiet Spirit: Amish Quilts from the Collection of Cindy Tietze and Stuart Hodosh* (Los Angeles: UCLA Fowler Museum of Cultural History, 1996), 19.

⁵ John A. Hostetler, *Amish Society*, 4th ed., (Baltimore: Johns Hopkins University Press, 1993), 82-84; Donald B. Kraybill, T*he Riddle of Amish Culture* (Baltimore: Johns Hopkins University Press, 1989), 95-99; Donald B. Kraybill, "Quiltwork," 17.

⁶ Patricia T. Herr, "What Distinguishes a Pennsylvania Quilt," in *In the Heart of Pennsylvania Symposium Papers*, ed. Jeannette Lasansky (Lewisburg, Pa.: Oral Traditions Project, 1986), 28-37; Eve Wheatcroft Granick, *The Amish Quilt* (Intercourse, Pa.: Good Books, 1989), 29-34, 75; Jonathan Holstein, "In Plain Sight: The Aesthetics of Amish Quilts," in *A Quiet Spirit: Amish Quilts from the Collection of Cindy Tietze and Stuart Hodosh* (Los Angeles: UCLA Fowler Museum of Cultural History, 1996), 76.

⁷ Patricia T. Herr, "Quilts Within the Amish Culture, in *A Quiet Spirit: Amish Quilts from the Collection of Cindy Tietze and Stuart Hodosh* (Los Angeles: UCLA Fowler Museum of Cultural History, 1996), 46-48; Granick, *Amish Quilt*, 31-32.

⁸ Barbara Brackman, *Clues in the Calico* (McClean, Va.: EPM Publications, 1989), 123.

⁹ Granick, *Amish Quilt*, 31; Holstein, "In Plain Sight," 83.

¹⁰ Granick, *Amish Quilt*, 73-150; Holstein, "In Plain Sight," 84-105; Hughes, *Art of the Quilt*, 23-24.

¹¹ Patsy Orlofsky and Myron Orlofsky, *Quilts in America* (New York: McGraw-Hill, 1974), 299.

¹² Amelia Peck, *American Quilts and Coverlets in the Metropolitan Museum of Art* (New York: Dutton Studio Books, 1990), 80.

¹³ Joe Cunningham, "Convention and Innovation in Amish Quilts," in *Amish Quilts 1880 to 1940 from the Collection of Faith and Stephen Brown* (Ann Arbor: University of Michigan Museum of Art, 2000), 25.

¹⁴ Granick. *Amish Quilt*.

¹⁵ Sara Laurel Holstein, "Sewing and Sowing: Cultural Continuity in an Amish Quilt," in *American Artifacts: Essays in Material Culture*, ed. Jules David Prown and Kenneth Haltman (East Lansing: Michigan State University Press, 2000), 103.

¹⁶ Holstein, "In Plain Sight."

¹⁷ Rachel Pellman and Kenneth Pellman, *Amish Crib Quilts* (Intercourse, Pa.: Good Books, 1985), 6.

¹⁸ The provenance is weak for most of the quilts, a limitation in being able to assign symmetry preferences to specific settlements. Eighty-seven per cent have been assigned a probable settlement and/or state. The breakdown by states is as follows: Ohio (26), Indiana (15), Iowa (14), Illinois (10), Kansas (6), Wisconsin (4), Michigan (2), Pennsylvania (1). For 10 quilts, the maker's name is known.

¹⁹ *Webster's New Universal Unabridged Dictionary*, 2nd ed., s.v. "symmetry."

²⁰ Peter S. Stevens, *Handbook of Regular Patterns* (Cambridge, Mass.: MIT Press, 1980), 18.

²¹ Definitions and explanations for symmetry analysis are derived from Dorothy K. Washburn and Donald W. Crowe, *Symmetries of Culture* (Seattle: University of Washington Press, 1988).

²² Ibid., 14-41.

²³ Dorothy Washburn, "Perceptual Anthropology: The Cultural Salience of Symmetry," *American Anthropologist 101* (1999): 553.

²⁴ Ibid., 553.

²⁵ Washburn and Crowe, *Symmetries of Culture*, 24.

²⁶ Carol Bier, "Elements of Plane Symmetry in Oriental Carpets," *Textile Museum Journal 31* (1992): 53-70; Carol Bier, "Symmetry and Pattern: The Art of Oriental Carpets," Textile Museum and Math Forum, 1997, http://mathforum.org/geometry/rugs/.

²⁷ Lynne B. Milgram, "The Textiles of Highland Luzon, Philippines," *Ars Textrina 18* (1992): 63-99; Priscilla A. Reinhardt and Linda Welters, "Symmetry Analysis of Embroideries on Greek Women's Chemises," *Clothing and Textile Research Journal 17*, no. 4 (1999): 176-90; V. Milasius, D. Neverauskienė, and I. Kazlauskienė, "The Mathematical Basis of Ornamentation of Lithuanian Patterned Woven Fabrics," *Ars Textrina 34* (2000): 1-13; T. Tantiwong, T. Cassidy, and M. A. Hann, "Symmetry in Thai Textile Patterns," *Ars Textrina 33* (2000): 1-28.

²⁸ Marie Jean Adams, *System and Meaning in East Sumba Textile Design: A Study in Traditional Indonesian Art*, Cultural Report Series No. 16 (New Haven: Yale University Southeast Asia Studies, 1969).

²⁹ Washburn and Crowe, *Symmetries of Culture*; Stevens, *Handbook*. Numerous mathematics and geometry websites use quilts to explore symmetry.

³⁰ Jinny Beyer, *Designing Tessalations: The Secrets of Interlocking Patterns* (Chicago: Contemporary Books, 1999).

³¹ Washburn and Crowe, *Symmetries of Culture*, 262.

³² Bier, "Elements of Plane Symmetry," 66.

³³ http://mathforum.org/geometry/rugs/.

³⁴ Bier, "Elements of Plane Symmetry," 66.

³⁵ Washburn and Crowe, *Symmetries of Culture*, 252, 255.

³⁶ Eight quilts were designed in variations of the strip format – Plates 9, 13, 19, 54, 58, 64, 66, 80, but only one had regular repeating patterns in the strips and could be classed as a one-dimensional pattern. Two additional quilts had motifs that repeated only once, qualifying them as one-dimensional patterns rather than finite designs (Plates 6 and 67).

³⁷ For the classifications of two-color designs, see Washburn and Crowe, *Symmetries of Culture*, chapters 3 and 5.

³⁸ Five quilts displayed $p_c'4mm$ patterns. The other five quilts were unique color arrangements: $c'm$, cmm', pmm', $p4m'm'$, and $p4'mm'$.

³⁹ Granick, *Amish Quilt*, 135. Granick's book is based on solid research: interviews, court records, and examination of "thousands" of quilts. She does not tell us how many quilts she examined in each of the communities included in her study. Thus, we do not know the basis for her conclusions about regional styles.

⁴⁰ For examples of Center Diamond quilts of Lancaster County, see the following: Rachel Pellman and Kenneth Pellman, *World of Amish Quilts* (Intercourse, Pa.: Good Books, 1984), 12-19; Hughes, *Amish Quilt*; Silber and Granick, *Amish Quilts of Lancaster County*.

⁴¹ Washburn, "Perceptual Anthropology," 552.

⁴² Pellman and Pellman, *World of Amish Quilts*, 102-03, 118-19; Pellman and Pellman, *Crib Quilts*, 95.

⁴³ Granick, *Amish Quilt*, 14-18, 31.

⁴⁴ Kraybill, "Quiltwork," 19-20.

BIBLIOGRAPHY

Adams, Marie Jean. *System and Meaning in East Sumba Textile Design: A Study in Traditional Indonesian Art.* Cultural Report Series No. 16. New Haven: Yale University Southeast Asia Studies, 1969.

Beyer, Jinny. *Designing Tesselations: The Secrets of Interlocking Patterns.* Chicago: Contemporary Books, 1999.

Bier, Carol. "Elements of Plane Symmetry in Oriental Carpets." *The Textile Museum Journal* 31 (1992): 53-70.

— "Symmetry and Pattern: The Art of Oriental Carpets." The Textile Museum and The Math Forum, 1997. <http://mathforum.org/geometry/rugs/> (7 October 2002).

Boynton, Linda. "Recent Changes in Amish Quiltmaking." *Uncoverings 1985.* Edited by Sally Garouette. San Francisco: American Quilt Study Group (1986): 33-46.

Brackman, Barbara. *Clues in the Calico.* McClean, Va.: EPM Publications, 1989.

Cunningham, Joe, and Eve Wheatcroft Granick. *Amish Quilts 1880 to 1940 from the Collection of Faith and Stephen Brown.* Ann Arbor: University of Michigan Museum of Art, 2000.

Granick, Eve Wheatcroft. *The Amish Quilt.* Intercourse, Pa.: Good Books, 1989.

Haders, Phyllis. *Sunshine and Shadow: The Amish and Their Quilts.* Clinton, N.J.: Main Street Press, 1976.

Havig, Bettina. *Amish Kinder Komforts.* Paducah, Ky.: American Quilter's Society, 1996.

Herr, Patricia T. "What Distinguishes a Pennsylvania Quilt." In *In the Heart of Pennsylvania Symposium Papers.* Edited by Jeannette Lasansky. Lewisburg, Pa.: Oral Traditions Project, 1986.

Holstein, Jonathan. *American Pieced Quilts.* New York: Viking Press, 1973.

Holstein, Sara Laurel. "Sewing and Sowing: Cultural Continuity in an Amish Quilt." In *American Artifacts: Essays in Material Culture.* Edited by Jules David Prown and Kenneth Haltman. East Lansing: Michigan State University Press, 2000.

Hostetler, John A. *Amish Society.* 4th ed. Baltimore: Johns Hopkins University Press, 1993.

Hughes, Robert. *Amish: The Art of the Quilt.* New York: Alfred A. Knopf, 1990.

Kraybill, Donald B. *The Riddle of Amish Culture.* Baltimore: Johns Hopkins University Press, 1989.

Kraybill, Donald B.; Patricia T. Herr; and Jonathan Holstein. *A Quiet Spirit: Amish Quilts from the Collection of Cindy Tietze and Stuart Hodosh.* Los Angeles: UCLA Fowler Museum of Cultural History, 1996.

Kraybill, Donald B., and Marc A. Olshan, eds. *The Amish Struggle with Modernity.* Hanover, N.H.: University Press of New England, 1994.

Milasius, V.; D. Neverauskiene; and I. Kazlauskiene. "The Mathematical Basis of Ornamentation of Lithuanian Patterned Woven Fabrics." *Ars Textrina* 34 (2000): 1-13.

Milgram, B. Lynne. "The Textiles of Highland Luzon, Philippines." *Ars Textrina* 18 (1992): 63-99.

Nolt, Steven M. *A History of the Amish.* Intercourse, Pa.: Good Books, 1992.

Orlofsky, Patsy, and Myron Orlofsky. *Quilts in America.* New York: McGraw-Hill, 1974.

Peck, Amelia. *American Quilts and Coverlets in the Metropolitan Museum of Art.* New York: Dutton Studio Books, 1990.

Pellman, Rachel, and Kenneth Pellman. *Amish Crib Quilts.* Intercourse, Pa.: Good Books, 1985.

— *The World of Amish Quilts.* Intercourse, Pa.: Good Books, 1984.

Reinhardt, Priscilla A., and Linda Welters. "Symmetry Analysis of Embroideries on Greek Women's Chemises." *Clothing and Textile Research Journal* 17, no. 4 (1999): 176-90.

Schlabach, Theron F. *Peace, Faith, Nation: Mennonites and Amish in Nineteenth-Century America.* Scottdale, Pa.: Herald Press, 1988.

Silber, Julie, and Eve Wheatcroft Granick. *Amish Quilts of Lancaster County.* San Francisco: M. H. de Young Memorial Museum, 1990.

Stevens, Peter S. *Handbook of Regular Patterns.* Cambridge, Mass.: MIT Press, 1980.

Tantiwong, T.; T. Cassidy; and M. A. Hann. "Symmetry in Thai Textile Patterns." *Ars Textrina* 33 (2000): 1-28.

Washburn, Dorothy. "Perceptual Anthropology: The Cultural Salience of Symmetry." *American Anthropologist* 101 (1999): 547-62.

Washburn, Dorothy K., and Donald W. Crowe. *Symmetries of Culture.* Seattle: University of Washington Press, 1988.

Wass, Janice Tauer. *Illinois Amish Quilts: Sharing Threads of Tradition.* Springfield: Illinois State Museum, 2002.

Weaver-Zercher, David. *The Amish in the American Imagination.* Baltimore: Johns Hopkins University Press, 2001.

ABOUT THE AUTHORS

Janneken Smucker is the Graduate Curatorial Assistant for the International Quilt Study Center at the University of Nebraska-Lincoln. She expects to complete her Master of Arts degree in Textile History and Quilt Studies with a minor in Museum Studies from the University of Nebraska-Lincoln in May 2003. Her research interests include Amish and Mennonite quilts and quiltmakers, intercultural aspects of material culture, and Anabaptist history. She was a 2002 scholarship recipient from both the Lincoln Quilters' Guild and the American Quilt Study Group.

Patricia Cox Crews is Director of the International Quilt Study Center at the University of Nebraska-Lincoln and Professor in the Department of Textiles, Clothing and Design. She served as primary editor for *Nebraska Quilts and Quiltmakers* (University of Nebraska Press, 1991), which won the Smithsonian's Frost Prize for Distinguished Scholarship in American Crafts in 1993. More recently she edited the exhibition catalogue *A Flowering of Quilts* (University of Nebraska Press, 2001).

Her research interests include American textile history, particularly American quilts and 19th century dyeing and printing techniques. Her research also focuses on textile conservation issues, including the lightfastness of natural dyes and environmental effects on museum textiles.

Linda Welters is Professor in the Textiles, Fashion Merchandising and Design Department at the University of Rhode Island. Her research interests include American quilts, archaeological textiles, and European folk dress. She edits *Dress*, the scholarly journal of the Costume Society of America. She co-edited and contributed to *Down by the Old Mill Stream: Quilts in Rhode Island* (Kent State University Press, 2000). Welters directed the Rhode Island Quilt Documentation Project, which won an Award of Merit from the American Association of State and Local History in 2001. She was a Visiting Faculty Fellow at the International Quilt Study Center for the 2002-2003 academic year.